UNIVERSAL RELIGION &
THE PSYCHIC FORCES

UNIVERSAL RELIGION
&
THE PSYCHIC FORCES

SOUMYADIPTA CHATTERJEE

Motilal Banarsidass Publications

MOTILAL BANARSIDASS
PUBLICATIONS
4741/23, Ansari Road, Daryaganj, New Delhi - 110002 (India)
Email: *mlbd@mlbd.com* | *sales@mlbd.com* | *exports@mlbd.com*
Website: *www.mlbd.com*

Universal Religion & The Psychic Forces
by
Soumyadipta Chatterjee

First Edition Published in 2022

Published in India by Motilal Banarsidass Publications

ISBN : 978-93-91759-17-9 (HB)

Printed and bound in India

ॐ

'Satyam Shivam Sundaram'
'Truth is beauty; Truth is Shiva'

Author's Note

"None becomes a Shiva Yogi without complete Samarpan, No Song is sung without soulfulness, No Yogi becomes a warrior without fierceness, no warrior becomes a King without leadership, no king becomes Shri Rama without Maryada, No Devotee becomes Shri Hanuman without divine love & None becomes Shri Krishna without Completeness".

Hare Krishna

It is a matter of great research, study, and experience before we write an entire document or a book on what religion is and how scientific it is.

Before I begin with such a book, it is therefore essential to justify for writing such a book. As a young **Computer Engineer** living in the **United States,** I may be entitled to write a book on automated software systems, complex codes & business processes. However, the fact that I chose to write beyond those technicalities of a material life signifies the exploration abilities of the mind & its analytical, scientific abilities beyond the known.

Explorers must attempt to know the unknown & through their constant research focus on bringing out the truth. Certainly, the uncertainty alone in this universe is the force that drives all our minds right from birth to death where we are obvious that there is something in our life which we all cannot deny especially when each day we can feel it.

Hence, I thought to write a book on this psychic/mystic

forces, which is absolutely beyond doubt affecting all our earthly mortal lives & driving us towards transformation.

Please consider the examples given below that will strengthen the feeling of this force.

- A student appearing for a competitive examination with a good preparation does not know how much rank range he will fall before the results are out. We call this exam luck in plain terms.
- A shipwrecked person does not really know up to which time he will survive if a help does not arrive. His life is entirely dependent on the balance between hope & anxiety. If he loses hope, he dies in seasickness.
- A person declared dead by doctors comes back to life and shocks all. The phenomenon remains unexplained, and doctors call it miracle.

Reference: - Val Thomas medical miracle case in West Virginia.

Therefore, as an engineer, as an astrologer, as a religious Brahmin mind and a practitioner of chiromancy I have tried exploring this force and understand its worldly existence in different forms. Therefore, while writing this book a significant transformational journey was undertaken by my mind & body to help understand readers from similar simplified backgrounds with the help of religion, science, philosophy & classify their cosmic life as a periodic dance of energy or a vibration.

By the time I have started writing this book I have already visited the Char-Dham or the four most sacred pilgrimages of Vishnu in Hinduism. The temples of Badrikashram,

Dwarika, Tirupati, and Puri. I have also seen eight of the twelve jyotirlingas of Lord Shiva. I have seen the pilgrimage of Pushkar where the only Brahma temple of the world is situated. I have seen the footprints of Lord Rama in the sacred temple of Rameswaram at TamilNadu and the birthplace of lord Hanuman at the Anjani Parvat in the Indian state of Maharashtra. I have bathed in the sacred waters of Ganga at Hardwar and Banaras and in the Sangam (meeting place of three great rivers) at Allahabad during Kumbha. This journey of development of the spiritual mind started early in my childhood when my Brahmin parents taught me religion and my career science & technology.

I was born and brought up in **Calcutta**, West Bengal, India the Land of **Swami Vivekananda**. Eventually I migrated to **Hyderabad, Telangana, India** and then **Mumbai, Maharashtra, India** for my work in & finally I immigrated to the **United States** & started living there at **Silicon Valley, California** where this psychic force and vision led me to. Each time I visited a place I have realized that this universe has a plan for me, and I got an initial vision and an urdent desire to visit the same before I went on and started living there physically.

This realization reached its pick when I visited Saturn temple at Shani-Shignapore village in **Maharashtra, India** and felt this great power.

Hence, religion, spirituality as well as science has a deep connection with respect to my existence. Having understood & comprehended that this psychic force exists in the forms we call Shakti in this universe, this book is an attempt to explore & compile these psychic forces as seen through the eyes of **Sanatan Dharma**.

I hope that I am serving as a medium as to what this universe wants to say. I often remember **Kekule** & his dream of a snake biting his tail, which led to the discovery of the atomic structure of benzene and is one of the most startling inventions. Somehow, universe helped in the above cause that is all we can say. Thus, the birth of a dream is the result of the conspiracy of the universe.

This book is therefore the result of a dream and is based on the facts, evidence, and the information that I have collected along with some of the startling explanations to our ancient Hindu mythologies, Astrology theorem and History along with a few of my personal experiences.

Please note that this book is for both the believers as well as the non-believers. I believe Theism is based on faith and atheism on facts. Human beings can be a machinery of faith and known as believers or they can be a machinery of constant scientific evolution & possess the power of wisdom to ask meaningful & right questions and be known as non-believers.

Hence, I leave it entirely up to the readers to measure the facts while reading and applying their minds. In this book, I have tried exploring both the faith and the facts and leave it up to the readers to express what they feel.

Sincerely,

Soumyadipta Chatterjee

Introduction

Shri Krishna in the Bhagvada Geetha Says:

> *amānitvam adambhitvam ahinsā kṣhāntir ārjavam*
> *āchāryopāsanaṁ śhauchaṁ sthairyam ātma-vinigrahaḥ*
> *indriyārtheṣhu vairāgyam anahankāra eva cha*
> *janma-mṛityu-jarā-vyādhi-duḥkha-doṣhānudarśhanam*
> *asaktir anabhiṣhvaṅgaḥ putra-dāra-gṛihādiṣhu*
> *nityaṁ cha sama-chittatvam iṣhṭāniṣhṭopapattiṣhu*
> *mayi chānanya-yogena bhaktir avyabhichāriṇī*
> *vivikta-deśha-sevitvam aratir jana-sansadi*
> *adhyātma-jñāna-nityatvaṁ tattva-jñānārtha-darśhanam*
> *etaj jñānam iti proktam ajñānaṁ yad ato nyathā*

This means

"Humbleness; freedom from hypocrisy; non-violence; forgiveness; simplicity; service of the Guru; cleanliness of body and mind; steadfastness; and self-control; dispassion toward the objects of the senses; absence of egotism; keeping in mind the evils of birth, disease, old age, and death; non-attachment; absence of clinging to spouse, children, home, and so on; even-mindedness amidst desired and undesired events in life; constant and exclusive devotion toward Me; an inclination for solitary places and an aversion for mundane society; constancy in spiritual knowledge; and philosophical pursuit of the Absolute Truth—all these I declare to be knowledge, and what is contrary to it, I call ignorance".

The Kalyuga or the dark age is not only the age of ignorance and passion, but it is the age of sin. What can be the greatest sin than deceiving oneself and abandoning one's faith. Demolishing one's faith to promote an era of materialistic pursuit is driving mankind in serious problems of anger, depression, anxiety, stress, and shorter life span. As the Kalyuga stands eye to eye with humanity it has destroyed all the ancient cultures of the world. Kalyuga or the dark age is a psychic force and extends much beyond our physical realities. Its roots are much deeper across all our incarnations and reincarnations. As the time passes its roots are becoming stronger. The question then comes to the mind that how do we preserve our spirituality? The answer has been given in the Bhagvada Geetha the song of the God. If we pursue the principle of Bhakti Yoga our hopes and chances increase. We can be rescued from the powerful claws of the Kaliyuga by this principle of Yoga.

In the modern world the true meaning of Yoga has lost its value. It has just been reduced to Asanas and Mudras which provides comfort to the human body in the form of exercises. The true spiritual meaning of Yoga of uniting oneself with the divine has lost. The world seldom realizes that a true Yogi is not the one who demonstrates Pranayama or Asanas on a global platform. All the scientists, Warriors& Leaders emerge from the principles of this Yoga alone. It's time that through the attempt of this book we will open the eyes of the world that how Yoga makes people an accomplished leader in any field whether material or spiritual. That Leader in its truest spiritual form is known as a Yogi.

The question that comes next to the mind is how we scientifically demonstrate and prove that this universe is an infinite vast ocean of Knowledge and Action and connect the messages of Bhagvada Geethato perceive knowledge and action as fruits of Gyan Yoga and Karma Yoga. The answer lies deeper within our consciousness.By identifying & studying the psychic forces that governs each of the deeper uncertainties of our lives we break the ice. We demonstrate that there is a realm beyond the predictable framework of science. We will also demonstrate that science is nothing but an inner Tantric Yoga which implements the principle of Samkhya Yoga, Gyan Yoga and Karma Yoga. Our approach throughout this book will thus be scientific and we will explain the divine psychic forces through the lens of the science. Thus, this book is for the humanity and restores Yoga its true value. This book prepares the mind to pursue Bhakti Yoga to know the unknown and explain them scientifically as the dance of Shakti. This book thus is a transformational journey from an ordinary human mind to a more spiritual Yogic mind and consciousness.

When the spiritual consciousness is developed the human mind knows and identifies their divine v/s demonic attributes and thus through the path of self-realization one purifies one's actions through the detachment of action to the fruit of it. This book identifies the universal psychic forces and how to work with them to create the Yogic consciousness. This book thus serves as a mirror as seen through the lens of Sanatan Dharma or Universal Religion.

When one sees the reflection of the light of Paramatma in every living being, the knowledge about Parambrahma enlightens that, Yogi. The knowledge of the Parambrahma liberates the searching mind and the Yogi reaches its destiny. This is the sole purpose of the Yoga. Yoga creates true human beings not mere objects of flesh and blood and sense gratifications.

With Love, Devotion and complete surrender can one dissolve themselves in true Bhakti. Its then that a human being realizes that his finite knowledge is like a differential in the mathematical language of Calculus. The differential Calculus is the principle of division of the human consciousness and the integral Calculus is the Yoga.Gravity and Magnetism are identified as Shakti in such a state of consciousness, and one realizes that one's true self lies in the transcendence and awakening of a journey beyond the physical and metaphysical realities, beyond incarnations and reincarnations.

The Journey of the Soul is eternal and true liberation lies in understanding and accepting this reality. This book prepares the mind and heart for an eternal journey and thus this book works on inclusiveness rather than exclusiveness. By overcoming the uncertainties and knowing the unknown human consciousness expands. This book's uniqueness lies in scientifically exploring the psychic forces and then let readers decide their existences in their own lives.

This book has been divided into seventeen sequential step by step chapters in the discovery of the spiritual truth. The first chapter discusses about the cosmic science that led to the creation and sustenance of this universe. The second chapter distinguishes the difference between the religion and spirituality and acts as a bridge between these two mountains. The third chapter is about the journey of the soul across various reincarnations and whatare subtle realms that exists. The fourth chapter identifies the Brahma and the Brahman and how they are connected. The fifth chapter discussed about Shri Vishnu and his Avatars. The Sixth chapter discusses about how a Shiva Yogi can find the ultimate truth in Lord Shiva. The seventh chapter discussed about the absolute universal vibration called Paramatma. The ninth chapter discusses about the Moksha and its various aspects. The tenth chapter is about the masculine and feminine forms of energies in the form of Purusha and the Prakriti. This chapter is an attempt to study the nature and how its feminine energy nourishes our Yogic mind. The eleventh chapter is very important and helps in understanding how astrology works under the light of the cosmic science and Yoga. The twelfth chapter is how self-realization can be achieved through Kundalini psychic force. The thirteenth chapter is where the specialty of this book lies as it maps the twenty-seven nakshatras or the constellations to the various heavenly realms. This chapter also discusses about hells and how the lower subtle worlds are related to them. The fifteenth chapter is finally about Kaliyuga and our role in this age. The sixteenth chapter is an excellent discussion on the universal form or Vishwaroopam or Virat Rupa of Shri Krishna. This chapter connects our existences and this universe to this universal divine form.Finally, the seventeenth chapter discusses the significance of the caring and that care that an enlightened soul can give and receive from the cows and other Jivatmas.

The lucid examples and explanations given in each chapter will awaken the consciousness, love, and attention of the readers while they go through this book.

At the end I pray to the Almighty that his fragrance and the tune of his flute spreads in every direction and language that the message of this book spreads.

His Humble Servant,

Bhagvada Das,
Soumyadipta Chatterjee

CONTENTS

1. The Zero and the Infinite and the beginning of a universe

Right from the beginning of the creation of human life the factor that has dominated the human mind is an irregularity, which has led to several discoveries over time. After man became civilized and left the nomadic life, studies have been performed by bright human minds over years to understand the purpose of existence. Science and technology have supported these causes and we have eliminated many superstitions as if the world is flat. Alas, the world is indeed round, and we are all connected to each other! Indeed, the discovery of fire and the fact that the world is not flat are the two significant discoveries of humankind since its origin. While the discovery of fire is age old, the other theory that the world is round is recent and ranges within 3000 years.

However, when the human mind has tried to search for the origin of the universe several challenges has come up in the path. Science is a theory based on experimentation, observation and inference and makes extensive usage of technology & mathematics to answer the rising questions. On the other hand, Philosophy is the study of general and fundamental problems such as those connected with reality, existence, knowledge, values, reason, mind, and language. While philosophy is logical and argument-based science is based on proof. When science addresses the fundamental problems, of life like the creation of the universe, philosophy must be strengthened and the bridge between science and philosophy must be formed to answer such questions. Neither science nor philosophy alone can answer such questions. While philosophy is based on the richness of the mind and is supported by a timely vision, science is fact based and helps philosophy to go a step forward and prove its theorem. Therefore, I have tried uniting both the science and the philosophy in understanding the concepts of zero, infinity & the universe and explaining them. Throughout this book, I will extensively use metaphysics for the explanation and understanding of the topics under discussion.

Now starting with religion and the relation of the universe with religion specially Sanatan Dharma the below fact is considerable.

Sanatan-dharma is not only a religion, but also a distinct research work by sages(scholars) over the ages based on the philosophy and sciences of those times and provides an answer to most of the startling questions. We will therefore explore our journey towards Hinduism and find the above in due course.

Beginning with **zero** the first thing that comes to the mind is the arithmetic notation '0' a big hollow round. Brahmagupta first laid down the concrete mathematical usage of zero in India in his book *Brhmasphuta-siddhanta* along with the computations of zero with the positive and the negative numbers. The big hollow round signifies the void or the vacuum and is a symbolic/notational representation of non-existence or something, which is missing or not present. In other words, zero is the symbolic notation of the state of the mind when an existing physical quantity does not exist.

Now if we add a whole /undivided quantity to zero we get something from a total nonexistent to something existing. If we go on adding whole numbers one by one over the vastness of time to the zero, a significant state of mind arises where our vision can no longer reach the vastness of the point of time where the count of a physical quantity becomes so large that it becomes immeasurable. We call this infinite denoted by '∞'. Thus, time plays an important role during the growth or withering.

Thus, a finite/determinate and infinite/indeterminate are two states of the mind where time itself should be determinate/indeterminate.

Now the question of growth towards infinity comes when the entity is in the process of acquiring. We denote this with the help of '+' sign in arithmetic/algebra. When an entity is in the process of growth towards infinity it should go on gradually acquire matter/length with time.

While during withering from an infinite existence to a zero existence, the same entity should pass through a phase of loss/ degeneration of the acquired matter/length with time. We denote this in arithmetic/algebra with minus '-'sign. Thus, when an infinite system breaks it should give away gradually what it has acquired over the infinite length of time. Similarly, when an infinite system grows over the infinite length of time it should acquire to support its growth.

Now if we consider our Universe as an infinite system, we would be able to understand its cause and effect. The universe was created from a point or cosmos particle, which started expanding continuously thereafter thus becoming an infinite isolated system. Stephen Hawkins in his theorem has stated that universe is expanding continuously and that the densities of the galaxies of the ever-expanding universe have been found to be varying. This is the proof of the cosmic

3

inflation over the time. There are also several theories like the heat death/big crunch supporting the end of the universe in a single point. Research is still going on in the direction of the future of the universe and to understand its cause and effect. The big bounce theory states that this universe will continuously repeat the cycle of the big bang followed by big crunch. This predicts that this universe in the process of contraction can give rise to several universes in the process of big bang followed by continuous process of big crunch.

Thus, the formation and destruction of a universe itself is an infinite cycle, which can give birth to other infinite cycles of birth and death of other universes.

Thus, Multi universe exists, and this fact is supported by science. Thus, this infinite universe was born out of destruction of another infinite universe.

Thus, from the above discussion we have seen how our infinite universe is born from a void or zero or out of a cosmic big bang in the form of a cosmic vibration which later on became a point cosmic particle and started expanding. The Hindus call this cosmic vibration 'OM' represented by symbol ॐ. It is just like the notation of any cosmology quantity. Since our universe was born out of this cosmic vibration, we Hindus consider this as a divine vibration. Generally, the OM is symbolically and respectfully pronounced in hymns as a humming sound **'aum'** and is said to contain the vibrations of all the frequencies of the universe as is obvious from its origin. Hence the ॐ is the vibration of the supreme soul or the Brahman and has three elementary energies united & embracing all the living & non-living entities- Brahma Shakti, Vishnu Shakti, and Shiva

4

Shakti which acts on three different core aspects of life. Therefore, OM is the reflection of the absolute reality and has three sounds at the core of its creation *a* (*akāra*), *u* (*u-kāra*), *m* (*ma-kāra*), of which it consists of. A-kāra means form or shape like earth, trees, or any other object. U-kāra means formless or shapeless like water, air, or fire. M-kāra means neither formless nor shapeless but still exists like the dark energy of the universe. Hence, OM captures all the material as well as non-material aspects of this universe like solids, liquids, gases, and dark energy of this universe in a universal flavor.

The Birth of this universe had been described in the Brahmanda –purana. Thus, science has taken its seed in the fertile valleys and minds of the Asian people thousands of years ago. **Brahmanda** as the name itself signifies means the cosmic egg. Thus, the elliptical shape of the universe was known to the scholars of that age. Modern age science has come up with theories that the universe is closed and is elliptical in shape. Thus, we can find some linkage. In the beginning of the universe, there was neither space nor time only dark energy predominated. According to Brahmanda-purana the gunas sattva, rajas and tamas were in a state of equilibrium. According to science, the gravitational force ruled the universe in the beginning. It is not clear how the first gaseous elements were born out of this circulating energy. However, the theory of relativity of Einstein states that energy and mass are inter convertible explains this formation. Gravity had acted upon the expanding universes varying density of the dark matter. Thus, out of the interaction between the dark matters, gravitational force and dark energy gaseous substance like helium & hydrogen were born.

5

Thus, gases and dust particles were born. Since the universe was much denser, matter was packed much more tightly together making it easier for gases to reach the critical density necessary for it to collapse in on itself under gravity and ignite nuclear fusion. Thus, out of the nuclear fusion of gaseous elements stars are formed in the universe, which becomes the source of ignition by supplying heat and the light energy.

If any explosion occurs during fusion, in these proto, stars then molten mass of minerals is thrown out in great velocity and this mass eventually cools down and becomes solidified. The point where the gravitational force of the star due to its mass becomes equal to the centripetal force due to the velocity of the solidified matter, equilibrium is reached between both the forces and a planet is formed which starts revolving around the star due to its tangential force and inertia.

Thus, the importance of stars in the universe lies in the fact that they are the main source of light and without them, there cannot be metals. Without a star, a solar system is lifeless. Therefore, stars are the main source of light, which in turn is the main source of life.

We will discuss in more detail about the star formation in the below section. Consider the below rough model of the expanding universe.

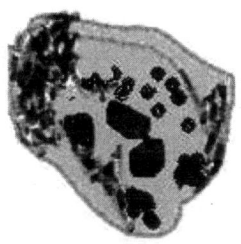

In the above picture, there are varying densities of the dark matter. The main process is governed by an imbalance between the gravity and pressure. At some point when a cloud of a dark matter condenses about a point a time arises when its internal pressure can no longer support its gravity/weight. Thus, it begins to collapse under gravity becoming smaller, denser, and hotter. This is referred to as the protostellar stage of a star where it is enshrouded by a natal envelope. The core is not fixed, and it is slowly spinning underweight.

Thus, when the rotatory motion becomes equal to the collapsing weight the star is born about its axis and due to fusion, light is radiated. Below is the illustrative image.

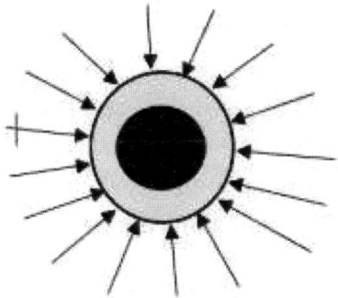

With the birth of the first star in the universe, time & space began. A star is a spherical body and gives rise to the dimensions of space and time. Thus, with the end of star in a black hole the space and time disappears. Thus, science explains the birth of the universe with the above explanations where the deep philosophy that light is born out of dark is involved. From M-kāra, both A-kāra and U-kāra are born and 'Aum' becomes complete manifesting all the energies and the vibrations of this universe.

Now the story of Brahmanda-purana goes like the Lord Brahma himself delivered this knowledge to the saints while they were on a sattara in the Naimisha forest. The hierarchy of deliverance is as below.

God Brahma → Sage Vasishta → Parasara→ Vyasa → Suta

According to the ancient story, Brahmanda purana was narrated by sage Suta, the disciple of sage Vyasa at the Naimisha forest to the saints upon their request. Vyasa delivered this knowledge to him and on the request to transfer; the knowledge of the creation and the gradual transmission of this universe Suta narrated it to the saints. Suta had a very humming voice along with a powerful presence and the deliverance of this purana made it clear of the knowledge of the entire Universe and its mysteries to the then world and its intellectual minds of India. Thus, Suta has reflected the power of knowledge in the sanatan-dharma (universal religion) or Hinduism and establishing the power of science at its base. The Naimisha forest is situated on the banks of the river Gomati, and it is a mystic place where the first narration of the Mahabharata took place.

Now we will see what Brahmanda-Purana has to say about the birth of the creation. At the beginning, the Brahman or the supreme soul of the universe constituting of three gunas

8

sattva, rajas and tamas was in a state of equilibrium. The supreme soul is called **Brahman** because it is very large (Brhat) in size, and it causes all the living beings to increase in size (ego). Thus, **Brahman** is the cosmic universal entity constituting of sattva gunas (attributes: gravitational force, stability formed by minimum energy state) bounding to creation, tamas gunas (attributes: dark matter, dry weight) and rajas gunas (attribute pressure difference, energy state difference) leading to motion. When this gunas were in a state of equilibrium, there was no creation. When the Gunas lost their equilibrium, the **Mahat** or great principle was born. The Mahat was predominated by gravity. **Hiranya** is the light life principle. He in whom this principle vibrates is **Hiranyagarbha.** Thus, Brahma or the Hiranyagarbha emerged with the birth of light or the first star of the universe and had four heads. The four heads are symbolic of the three space dimensions and one dimension of time. With the birth of Brahma, space and time were born and thus began creation.

The entropy of the universe slowly began to increase with the advent of the Brahma. With Brahma is also born the light of Knowledge or the Vedas. Therefore, in mythology the four heads of Brahma are the Vedas.

Thus, Brahma Shakti is the energy of the creation or the seed of the creation. Hence, Brahma resides on the lotus or the seed coming out of Vishnu's (the sustainer's) navel. Thus, Vishnu/sustenance nourishes Brahma/creation. Hence pictorially the umbilical cord is shown to come out of Vishnu's Navel and ending in a surrounding of lotus inside which the seed of creation/Brahma resides. Brahma Shakti is unborn and indestructible and needs to manifest itself in a stability or equilibrium of energy state. This is known as Vishnu Shakti. Hence, Vishnu is the sustainer or the stable energy state that preserves the equilibrium of the universe. When the equilibrium is slowly lost due to external/internal disturbance of energy level of the system, the stability is lost & the system degenerates or turns into new transition or decaying state. This unstable energy state known as Shiva Shakti or the truth. Since due to instability a system is created which ultimately proceeds towards stability and again gets destroyed this is known as Shiva or the ultimate truth. Thus, stability or the equilibrium is the main thing for which a system craves in this universe. During this process, a stable system might come in interaction of another stable system and another system is born out of their interaction, which might crave to be in more minimal energy state or stability. Thus, creation, sustenance/growth and destruction occur in a cycle and governed by three energy states Brahma Shakti, Vishnu Shakti and Shiva Shakti.

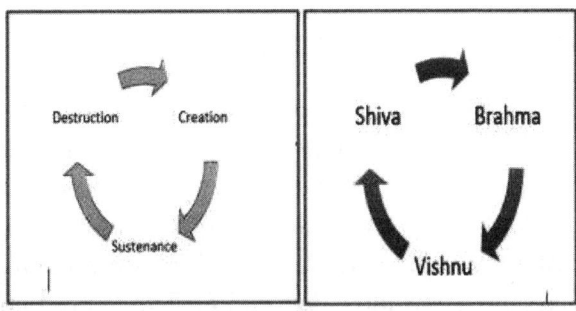

Brahma is associated with Rajas Guna or the passion (rising from difference in energy states), Vishnu resides in Sattva Guna (stable equilibrium state) and Rudra/Shiva resides in Tamas Guna (decaying state or the process of decaying). Thus, Vishnu lok can be attained only when the sattva Guna increases.

Now coming back to the science and philosophy bridge the stars of the universe and the creation cycle is described below.

Gradually with rising entropy stars started to take birth one after the other and thus were born the **Pancha Bhutas** or the elements of creation **Agni**(heat/fire), **Vayu**(gases), **Prithvi** (minerals/metals), **Jal**(water), **Akash** (interstellar space).

Since they are five in number, they are known as five elements of creation or Pancha Bhutas. All the living entities are composed of these elements.

If we observe the human body consists of blood/fluids, calcium/iron &other minerals, oxygenated/deoxygenated cells, heat generated due to oxidation of food and organic cavity. Hence, the human body is consisting of the **Pancha**

11

Bhutas, which are the main composition of its formation and structure.

With the birth of the planets and subsequent climatic changes, life started originating on a favorable planet, our earth. There have been several climatic changes due to which the Mountains gradually broke down and soil was formed. At first, the earth was a molten mass of fire and frequent volcanoes would cause molten lava to predominate the earth. The age was known as fire age. With the gradual slowdown of volcanic eruptions, the lava cooled. Due to fire, age there was heavy formation of water vapor.

From clouds, heavy rain down poured on earth. Hence, after fire age there was water age when the earth was submerged in water. With changing climate, the water gradually froze and ice age began. During the last cycle of the water age, the continents gradually emerge out of continuous water body. Thus, human life started on earth.

The history of Mankind has a story in Vedas that starts with Lord Vishnu taking the form of a boar and lifting the earth out of continuous water. That story is probably the one related to the emerging of the landmass out of ocean in geography due to tectonic movement of the earth plates.

The Brahmanda Purana states that at the beginning there was one vast ocean. This primeval watery flood expresses the infinite unmanifest cause of the universe. Brahma named Narayana with a thousand heads slept there. Narayan means *'the one who rests on water'*. The term Narayan has also several meanings and each meaning in different context can help identify the actual concept. It means 'he who is the dwelling place' meaning further the source, support, and dissolving ground of all jivas or souls. Thus, Brahma Shakti,

Vishnu Shakti and Shiva-Shakti are the three energy states of the supreme Narayana or the universal active energy. When this great energy/force of the universe was passive/inert during the course of equilibrium of the gunas (already explained in terms of science) the Narayan slept. He has thousand (innumerable) heads since all the living entities and the stars emanated from this great cosmic manifestation/loss of equilibrium. It is said he remained meditated there for thousand Yugas (infinite time during the origin of universe) remaining inert.

He moved alone in the waters and knew that universe had sunk in that vast expanse of the water and thought of an eightfold cosmic body in the beginning of the kalpas. Thus, he assumed the form of a boar, lifted the earth, and rearranged its mountains, oceans etc.

This story is thus symbolic and tells us that everything is born from this great ocean of **ether** including the stars, planets, and life on earth. Hence, Narayana assumed the form of Vishnu or growth/sustenance of land mass and like a boar (crane) helped the land mass to emerge.

The puranas are extensive source of rich literature and makes usage of distinct comparisons to deliver its subject. Hence, often the comparisons or representation becomes a puzzle and true matter depiction becomes difficult. However, with scientific attempts and an understanding of literature the meaning can be depicted/ decoded to find the factual truth.

The Brahmanda-purana gives the concept of Pralaya/dissolution and recreation and can be explored as below.

According to the purana, the Pralaya is of four types.

13

1) Nitya Pralaya or usual: It is what goes on everyday e.g., death of beings.

2) Naimittika Pralaya or periodical: It takes place at the completion of each Kalpa i.e., at the end of one thousand sets of Yugas. God Brahma begins to absorb the subjects in him. A continuous drought for thousand years goes on. The sun with its seven rays burns up everything and evaporates the oceans. The samvartaka clouds burn the world and then pour torrential rains, everything mobile and immobile is destroyed and dissolved into one vast expanse of water, and God Brahma becomes a thousand headed entity and goes to sleep for a period of one thousand sets of four Yugas. At the end of Brahma's night, he wakes up and recreates.

3) Prakritika Pralaya: It takes place at the end of Brahma's period. When the withdrawal of the universe is imminent elements both gross and subtle are annihilated. Evolutes of the Prakriti beginning with Mahat and ending with Visesas are destroyed. The waters swallow the special quality or smell of the earth. The fire up to the sky of the earth merges into bhutadi i.e., all the five elements of the creation dissolve and only atman or the soul remains. This principle is recurrent and probably refers to the destruction of a galaxy.

4) Atyantika Pralaya: It takes place when one becomes liberated through spiritual knowledge. He does not again take up a body. This is called dissolution due to drowning of knowledge.

Thus, when a soul attains moksha or liberation it dissolves into infinity again and he only consisting of sattva gunas dissolves in the equilibrium of the gunas in the most stable portion of the universe. All the material elements are dissolved and the soul merges into the equilibrium of the universe. There is always a portion of the universe which is stable and where all the instabilities will dissolve at the end of the universe and merge into one-point cosmos particle again.

Thus, the Brahmanda-Purana not only mentions about the creation but also the dissolution of the creation into the infinite.

Thus, at the end of this chapter we have understood the evolution of this infinite Brahmana or the universe, its basic elements and the three elementary psychic forces that drives our life- Brahma, Vishnu, and Shiva.
In the later portion of this book, I'll explore the details of this psychic forces and their existence in this universe in three different spiritual energy worlds known as Brahma Lok, Vishnu Lok, and Shiva Lok apart from their partial material existence into our own world.

2. Religion and Spirituality

While the birth of both spirituality and religion has its common roots in the deep faith inside the human heart, spirituality is more fact based, dynamic and often larger in life than religion. Religion has evolved from spirituality and the searching mind. Thus, with the evolution of human life began the search of absolute truth which took its seed in the origin and the history of religion.

With the evolution of religion, a new direction came to the human life, which helped humanity to test the strength of one's moral character, the values, and ethics of an individual and the integrity and evolution of human mind from its wild and savage nature to a more civilized and positive goal-oriented life. Religion is thus the basis of humankind, which in terms has evolved from spirituality. Whenever a religion thus reaches its saturation point, a spiritual person is born to add more values/paths to it and save it from the curse of destruction as per the universal theorem described in the first chapter. Thus, spirituality always saves religion from death and destruction and prevents it from decaying. Hence, Spirituality is the heart of every religion and without spirituality, a religion cannot survive.

A religion is often more process oriented and endorses a set of practices and procedures to fulfill its purpose. While spirituality is aimed at the individual liberation of a human being, a religion is aimed at the liberation of a human society and the methodologies, practices they can adapt in doing so. Thus, religion has a broader audience and is evolved once spirituality has established its theorem and proof in the deep hearts of the people.

A religion endorses the following main attributes in its existence.

- Faith
- Divinity
- Superstition
- Sacrificial procedures
- A symbolic representation/idol of the Divine personality
- Assembly hall for prayer/sacrifice
- Charitable causes and the assembly halls for them.
- Priests and set of devotees
- Scriptures or documents
- Festivals
- Traditional nature

I will explain these attributes in detail in the later portion of this chapter. However, it is important to understand the characteristics of spirituality as well. Although religion contains spirituality, the flavor of spirituality is completely different from religion.

The distinct attributes of spirituality therefore are as follows: -

- searching mind
- Strong desire to understand truth
- Self-explanatory
- Evolution
- Formless power (Param Brahm)
- Action driven realization (karma yoga)
- Intuitive and meditative
- Dynamic nature

Thus, although religion contains some components of spirituality, the two are very different elements and are the main gifts to the world by distinct human beings.

Lower creatures other than human beings may be spiritual but their evolution has not been able to gift a religion to the world. Thus, the birth of a religion is the most significant evidence of the spiritual advancements happening in human life and gradual evolution of the spirit.

Now let us consider the example of Lord Krishna to help us understand the concept of spirituality in the best possible manner. Krishna himself was more spiritual than religious and hence Krishna himself is a religion. Lord Rama was bounded by the rules of the society and hence was an incarnation of Maryada, however Shri Krishna is a complete incarnation of God and therefore he is the Universe & its Maryada himself. His mother Yashoda saw the ntire Brahmanda when she opened his mouth as a child upon being worried by seeing him putting mud into his mouth. Therefore he reformed the then society and destroyed its evil to sustain it in its positivity in the battle of Kurukshetra. Therefore Shri Krishna is a complete system in himself. Krishna has given his own theories of dharma and truth to the world and thus changed the concept of truth that was given by the earlier incarnation Lord Rama. Krishna abolished the worship of Lord Indra in Vrindavan, since Demi gods should not be worshipped out of fear. He asked humankind to worship demigods only in case of devotion and respect. Thus, Krishna was grossly spiritual in his approach. These principles were later endorsed in Sanatan dharma, which widened its horizon. Thus, spirituality is the main aspect of Sanatan Dharma.

With the advent of Ramakrishna Paramhans, the concept of spirituality became prominent in modern times. His inclusion of Swami Vivekananda, initially a non-Brahmin as his disciple and later Swamiji's establishment of Hinduism as a universal religion vandalized the age-old system of categorization in Hinduism and helped it emerge stronger. Thus, the spiritual Vivekananda laid the foundation of the Ramakrishna Mission which in itself is a separate religion providing a just cause to the society and its people.

The basic difference in religious and a spiritual person can be understood by the two perceptions of the same thing below.

"To a religious person a Brahmin is the one who takes birth in a Brahmin family and follows the occupation of performing the rituals of worshipping and other tasks in a domestic family/temple according to his family's occupation and considers his action/occupation as his birthright".

On the other hand, a spiritual person will consider the below perception.

"A true Brahmin is the one who understands the meaning of intellectuality and divine forces and chooses his profession according to these principles thus learning and understanding them which leads to the karma (action) that reflects his intellectual & true nature of his spirit".

Thus, the main basis of a spiritual human being is self-realization and his selection of karma that will lead him to the truth whereas the main basis of religion is following the century old traditions.

Thus, with time a religion must understand time's tide and modify/upgrade itself according to the demand of the age. Thus, in such times there is a friction between tradition and dharma. Thus, with the turning wheel of the time a Mahabharata is born during such frictions to resolve the conflict and to give birth to new traditions.

Spirituality is thus the dynamic aspect of a religion and helps it to align itself in the direction of the changing universe. We will now discuss in detail the various attributes of the religion. As mentioned above the fundamental aspect of religion is **Faith**.

There are several elements of spirituality –mystical experiences, transcendence, sanctification, spirituality as problem solving skill and spirituality as ethical and virtuous behavior. These are the components of spiritual intelligence.

Thus, when a person experiences mystical events he should not be afraid of the experiences but try to understand what the universe is trying to tell him through the sequence and have complete trust or faith in the universe and it's Lord.

Faith is unconditional based on complete belief without any prejudice. Faith is born from complete submission. When a creature completely submits itself to something, that something completely manifests itself in that living creature. Thus with faith one can attain god. **Faith** (belief) is the most powerful psychic force governing the **cause** and **effect** rule in this universe. Consider one living being strongly believing in something with infinite patience, that event after a substantial amount of time will definitely come true. This is because his faith will create an agitation among the gunas in the universe.

That agitation will propagate throughout the universe and

will result in loss of equilibrium of the gunas. This is the basis of the creation as already discussed. The stronger the faith the greater will be the agitation. Hence, his faith will take its form and will ultimately come forward. Thus, faith is the basis/origin of all actions.

Religion is thus born from a great faith. This was the faith in mystic power. The negative form of faith is Fear. When a human being negatively believes in something, it becomes fear. Thus, demons were born of negative faith or fear. Thus, divine, and demoniac attributes manifest itself strongly in positive or negative belief.

To some people the mystic powers are formless and to some they have form. Hence, they will give birth to religions either formless or with form. Thus, Sanatan Dharma was born with form.

In Hinduism, the gods are not formless and have pictorial depiction. This is because the gods have been either divine cosmic beings or their divinity have been represented through pictures, which has hidden meanings. For example, please consider the picture of lord **Narayana**. He is shown to rest in the infinite waters on a thousand headed serpent, goddess Laxmi sitting at his feet. He is gradually taking the form of Vishnu. Thus, he is shown to emerge with four hands holding lotus, conch shell, mace, and wheel. As already discussed, Narayana means the abode of rest of all the living creatures in the infinite universe. It is the nascent or the sleeping state of life. Hence, it is shown to rest. Since there are innumerable living souls manifesting and coagulating together waiting for Narayana to take form, they are represented as the hoods of the great serpent. The serpent itself is the nascent power from which the souls will degenerate into the material world or the world with formation. The serpent or the Ananta (infinite) nag represents the mysterious power surrounding Vishnu and coiling around him.

The Narayan when awake will become Vishnu or the sustained energy and hence is said to hold **lotus** symbolizing the creation and the purity of soul right at the basis of it, untouched by impurity and moving upwards towards enlightenment. The Vishnu holding the **wheel** symbolizes the mobility of time. The **Mace** in his hands symbolizes power and protection. The **Conch** symbolizes the announcement or the birth of the audible sound from the inaudible cosmic vibration and represents the purity of speech in living creatures. The goddess of prosperity Laxmi sitting at the base of his feet and serving him signifies that wealth, prosperity and lifestyle will serve the vital life energy manifesting itself in the highest form in human society. Hence Vishnu or the sustainer vital energy will always be reborn in the form of incarnation to teach ideal lifestyle & ethics to human beings in changing courses of time and will be the most powerful, prosperous, intelligent, benevolent, and just of all the human beings of his time.

His lotus or beautiful and pure feet will fill the entire earth with the beautiful fragrance of kindness, love, respect and benevolence towards the pure soul or the Brahmin, Cow and pious women and all the believers. Whereas he will be tough towards the chastisers, the unethical, the impatient and the misusers of the power of mind and soul leading to the destruction of their mortal body.

Therefore, the entire picture of Vishnu depicts that the creation or the soul untouched by impurity will move towards enlightenment and will be protected in the course of time and attain the highest power of mind and soul. The person with the highest power of mind will also be entrusted with the acts of protection, prosperity and soothing speech with the course of time to contribute towards the growth and sustenance of the society and vital life. This is the universal manifestation theory of the energy of sustenance (first law of thermodynamics) and the Hindus have given it a holy form of Lord Vishnu.

This represents the strongest faith on the universal theory of the sustenance (first law of thermodynamics) and seen to become true when Bhakta **Prahalad** believed strongly in this vital life energy of the protection. The formless took the form of **Nar Singh** (half man &half lion) and emerged out of a life less pillar to save his life from his demoniac father. Thus, Faith is the basis of creation, sustenance and forms the base of a religion and its mythology.

The Hindus strongly believe that god is not formless since they don't have a single god and by the term god, they understand the cosmic energy (**G**enerator **O**perator **D**estroyer) in all its elementary aspects which they have seen taking form from formless and hence they worship idols of those formations. Human beings who in their lifetime have manifested this vital energy have been identified by the scholars and have been given God hood in the Hindu religion. Lord Krishna and Rama are thus two such incarnations or Godhead in Hinduism.

After Faith forming the basis of a religion the key attribute that brings life to it are its **Divinity** or divine nature. The positive supernatural power surrounding us represents divinity. Hence, miracle, vision and soul are all divine. With the birth of the mind was also born **Maya** (illusion). Since the mortal mind cannot percept everything and interpret, we are obvious that it has limitations. Thus, illusion represents the confused state of mind or the state of mind when truth cannot be presented and interpreted as it is. This is where divinity and faith prevail which helps to clear the illusion and visualize truth. When this illusion is cleared with the help of faith, we call this a divine transcendence.

The next key attribute of a religion is **superstition**. Although superstition is not mentioned in any textbooks of a religion but still, I have considered it as an integral part of a religion. The reason for this consideration is again the Maya or the illusion of human mind. This illusion is sometimes so strong that the mind out of negative faith or fear derives theories known as superstitions. These are often not only false but are far away from truth.

Sacrificial procedures are those attributes of the religion, which are meant to render satisfaction to the demigods. Every natural force is worshipped as a demigod in Hinduism and are considered living entities. Hence, sacrifices or Yajnas are performed addressing the demigods to show respect and devotion. The sacrifices help in cleansing the negative karmas/actions and helps in the purification of mind and soul. Assembly halls for sacrifices or **ashrams** and **tapovans** used to exist for this purpose.

I have already explained the attribute of **Idol worship before**. Hence, we will discuss the **charitable** aspect of a religion in detail now.

The temples are the main centers where people come and offer their prayers. Often, they donate money to the temples, which are then accumulated and spent for distributing foods, clothes, and other services to the poor and the devotees of the religion. There are also **priests** of the temple whose family sustenance is dependent on the charitable donations of the devotees. Thus, the charitable aspect of a religion is essential as a large portion of the society is depending on the above. The poor, the beggar and the needy can be helped with the charitable purposes. It helps to spread the message of goodness to the weak portions and the needy people of the society, the religion and helps to restore their faith on Divine. A religion that does not have a charitable aspect indicates selfishness of mind and is soul less, ungrateful, and unkind. Such a religion cannot exist as we always owe our success and existence to our society and should therefore contribute towards its progress.

The **festivals** are the key aspects of a religion and are the moments of celebration where the society unites together and enjoy the auspicious day in a traditional manner. Often the festival dates are some memorable events in the history of the religion when its idols have strongly established its principles in the heart of the people. Those days are celebrated in every solar year to remember their importance and foster the same faith in the future generations. In India there are several festivals in a year and the happiness lasts in the people the entire year for each of them. Thus, religion ensures our happiness through celebration.

The Holy **scriptures** are the documents where the religion principles, science and philosophy have been recorded and preserved over the ages for future propagations to its population.

Now let us see how **spirituality** is helpful in realizing god and how a person who denies the presence of psychic forces and claims that he has done everything lies.

Such a type of person will never think deeply who he is and what he will be after his death. Any attempt of making him think will fail because his approach is in denying everything. He has already asked the eyes of his mind to close and will never open it until and unless he himself would like to. Such a person is only dependent on his present. When the present is good and yield results, he is happy. When the future changes into present and does not yield result, he is unhappy and spends his life in various forms of addiction. Waiting for the time again to change in and yield good results understanding that everything is not in his hands, realizing little that nothing is in his hands and denying that his existence is a play of cosmic energies which are inter transferrable into states of being alive, dead, active, and dormant. His exists based on the path of denial.

On the other hand, the existence of a **Yogi** is through acceptance. **Yoga** means integration and thus a Yogi is the one who integrates and accepts all the vibes of the cosmic energy of life into himself and treats them equal. Thus, a yogi treats both light and shade as two states of the same day and his state of mind is same for both of them. He does not crave for light; neither does he crave for shade. He accepts them as it is during his journey of life. Thus, a Yogi integrates all forms of life energy unto him, realizes the infinity or the infinite cosmic energy of the universe, and thus realizes god. The most realistic and practical example of a Yogi accepted worldwide would-be Jesus Christ who absorbed all the cosmic energy unto himself and thus declared the kingdom of heaven is open to all pure consciousness. The Bhagwat Gita also declares the same. God is waiting for us with his arms open, we just need to cleanse ourselves and knock his door with a pure consciousness. However, we are afraid to leap into the unknown infinity and thus we close our eyes in fear when we see the raging ocean of the infinite.

The raging ocean is just an illusion to test our perseverance and penance. When our consciousness is pure the Maya turns into truth and the raging ocean turns into the heavenly lake of **Man Sarovar**; the abode of thousand petal lotuses. Thus, with spirituality a Yogi gains his vision of integrating the truth in all forms of life and attains heaven or the eternal abode of happiness. The question is thus simple: what is spirituality? The answer is simple as well: spirituality is an attempt to be happy always by treating both happiness and sadness as equal by accepting them as two visions of the same life or two faces of the same coin. The person who keeps his balance in all states of life is a true Yogi and attains Moksha or liberation.

Thus, with the above notes' life can be classified as a play of spiritual and material energies. The person who is grossly spiritual realizes this truth and endorses materialistic energy (Maya) as only a part of the entire life cycle.

He tries to transform himself into a Yogi (a swan swimming on the infinite waters of the entire life energy of the universe). On the other hand, an ordinary human being is deeply drowning in the infinite sea of the life energy and the material energy circulates around him. He fails to swim like a swan. Thus, in course of time he is so deeply immersed that his consciousness fails to emerge, his mind become closed. Such a person does work but his action is always result oriented. When he achieves success, he stores and multiplies his material possession. When he fails, he becomes deeply distressed. However, when he regains his balance he again craves for a new result and this infinite accumulation play continues. God has given human beings life to celebrate this life.

However, such people spend their entire life for accumulating luxurious items for their home, family, and themselves. Little realizing that most time is spent accumulating luxury, and little spent in enjoying them. Thus, the inner growth of such an individual stops and he often regrets or complaints of petty things due to lack of enjoyment. Life starts becoming more difficult in keeping a handsome ratio between necessity and luxury. With time necessity increases and luxury replaces necessity. As slowly and slowly all the luxuries become necessity the hunger of the individual increases and he the material energy slowly takes over him. He thanks individuals, but he forgets to thank god.

On the other hand, some people with higher strata of spiritual energy utilizes this opportunity and thanks god for all the things that he gets, realizing that he owns nothing in this universe except his soul, his consciousness. With absolute knowledge comes humility and consciousness and a human being realizes that we all are co related in this universe and our growth (inner/outer) is due to the people around us. Either we can choose to thank these individuals, or we can choose to thank the god who has created these individuals. Indeed again, such people thank the Paramatma inside him, all and the inner growth of such individuals continues in any circumstances.

The idea here is that when material energy is slowly tightening its grip over the human being like a serpent our mind and soul undergoes a change. The soul becomes more tightly coupled in the internal desires and takes external manifestations in the form of birth and rebirth. In this way, the conditioned soul totally forgets the universal cosmic knowledge.

If we think deeply then we can understand that in the above condition it becomes very difficult to release one's grip over known things. This search for unknown and uncomfortable truth is of practically no use to such a person as he is looking and struggling for earning money to satisfy his needs and beyond.

American self-development bestselling books emphasize in using our positive energy for acquiring skills, which could lead us in earning more success & acquisition of wealth. Some of these books research on smiling & spreading its positive vibration to the other people around us and this produces magical effects. These research even teach us to appreciate other people in order to earn the same appreciation from them. The main theme of these books is to transform a human being by generating positive thinking habits, which can drive them to success. These books also state that what separates a successful person from an ordinary person is his way of thinking and managing himself. *Thus, in one way these books are highlighting the consciousness inside us, which can lead to success.*

Thus, these self-development books are simply using the para psychological principle of redirecting the spiritual energy to acquire wealth and success in the society. They are using stories of highly successful and wealthy people like **Henry Ford** as motivators.

Thus, by using the above American success formula we can see that several human beings are benefitted and that anyone can become rich and successful if he has the ardent desire to do so.

This is simply using your spiritual power for attaining your material desires. If these self-development books by American writers are getting practical results, then on the other handbooks like **Monk who sold his Ferrari** by an Indian writer are also drawing much attention because of its spiritual appeal.

Thus, the spiritual power is at the root of attaining everything. From a Ferrari, beautiful home, a wife, wonderful and passionate children, brilliant job and office surrounding, helpful neighbors to the moksha (spiritual healing), emancipation and universal (divine) knowledge, spiritual power is at the heart of everything.

When we say awakening the spiritual power it is like standing in front of the rising ocean that is about to crash during a tsunami and say Hello. The reason I used this metaphor is because the spiritual power is a vast ocean of infinity spread over this universe. We are just mere drops of this vast ocean however at the same time, we have the entire ocean inside us. Thus, the ocean outside is **Mahavishnu,** who created the entire material energy or **Mahat tattva.** The **Ksirodakasayi Vishnu or the Paramatma** is the inner ocean within us. Thus, when we as **Jivatmas (individual drops)** are able to diffuse with the Paramatma or **Ksirodakasayi Vishnu** we will be able to realize the **Mahavishnu.** The irony of the story is that we have both the thirst & the ocean to quench the thirst inside; however, we lack the knowledge to explore it within.

Thus, in order to explore this knowledge, I tried searching some of the answers to the biggest questions of human life. One of these questions was how do living beings convert their feelings of insecurity into security and how do they convert their fear into courage. These are essential for their survival, especially for those species, which are migrating. I found the answers to these questions in many forms. I happen to meet with many wonderful people, which I have deeply desired and found most of my answers.

In this era of globalization, in spite of the geographical and cultural diversity among the people they are working together as a team to accomplish a common goal towards their financial growth, their company and towards their country. People due to their jobs, business are migrating from their well-known small towns towards larger commercial metropolitan cities. These cities are becoming localized centers for trade, commerce, and jobs. People are migrating in larger numbers towards these places for earning bread and butter. Thus, their consciousness is transforming towards growth that is more material. Jobs are becoming 24X7 because the companies need to do business 24 hours for more money. Thus, the human beings are trapped in this system. Now every service is emergency service not just police, hospital, and fire brigade. Thanks to the booming **IT industry** and the great technological inventions of America, Indians are making money in exchange of their services. They are migrating from India to Europe, USA, Australia, Dubai and even Japan for bread and butter. Thus, IT has reduced the Geographical and cultural diversities and has united the entire globe for trade and commerce. This is a blessing for people as it created employment and opportunities for more financial growth. However, its greatest gift is uncertainty as the great service industry is flourishing on shares. When these shares fall people lose their job. Stock Markets come under recession. The crowd towards churches, temples and mosques increases and we can even see people taking holy bath in the pilgrimages for escaping their cruel fate. Taking loans from Bank to buy a flat in suburban has become a common culture in this era of capitalism.

The idea behind the above narration of the global movement is simple, I tried to visualize the movement of this age and find my answers. I could see that modern technology is hardly 200 years old and it will last hardly for another thousand years more. Everything is virtual and computerized in this age. Usage of Digital Currency made money become just a number to create digital assets. A rich man can become bankrupt suddenly if he doesn't know how to manage his digital assets. Similarly, an ordinary person can suddenly become a millionaire if he comes up with a new idea that can be digitized for commerce.

Thus, in this era of digitization we can see that migration (geographical/cultural) is a process of transformation and the development of an individual towards a wider growth.

Even if we sit at our fixed home, time will move, and the world will migrate and change. If the movement is towards growth we grow, thus the rotation of the globe affects us all. *In our life cycle, we try to convert our insecurity of survival into security by owning something.* We say our country, our land, our house, our company, our team, and it is insecurity that speaks in the form of 'our', 'us'. As individuals, we cannot achieve anything; we need to be **us** to achieve something. Again, we convert our fear into courage by acquiring something that gives us a base of ownership, a feeling of security and we find a meaning of our existence. This feeling is similar in animals as well. A lion defends his territory for the same feelings. A dog protects the house that it lives for the same feelings.

Thus, we all are born with the same flavor of spirituality in us and slowly transforms it in the direction that the divine energy wants us to be. That direction is acquiring responsibility. Spiritual beings also convert their insecurities and fear into a sense of deep security but differently. *They acquire responsibility and knowledge of knowing the unknown.*

3. The Duality or transition of spirit and the theory of rebirth

Transformation is what every creature goes through in different phases of life and the individual is reborn repeatedly in the same life. During my extensive journey through this phase, I have performed a significant & lengthy research on the psychological and cosmic aspects. I have wondered several times that if there can be several new lives among a single life then there is bound to be several new lives in a single death. Death is simply a transformation from a formed entity to a formless entity.

Transformation is again a journey from a known to an unknown manifestation.

That is where the word "**survival**" becomes so insignificant and hollow. Survival is a relative word & only significant when we are born. However, in the face of death, decay and transformation cosmic eternity replaces survival. Individuals will no longer fight for survival, as they are eternal. Thus, in one-way **rebirth** and **survival** are two points of an eternal transformation.

Here the **law of karma** for physical entities comes into the physical frame. The eternal law of **cause and effect** works on individuals during this process of transformation. The law of karma manifests in this universe through divine entities who have the universal responsibility of transformation through the dimension of time. Science & Astrology can visualize these divine entities in the form of stars & planets. There are two categories of planets according to Astrology. These are benefic & malefic planets respectively. Both have their own significance in this universe and are required for maintaining the balance. People are afraid of the malefic planets without understanding the core concept. The astrologers suggest remedy to escape the wrath of such planets to the clients. However, such remedies if not properly followed from the inner consciousness will not help much.

I will reveal the deepest of the secrets to my readers today based on the law of Karma. Malefic planets will act on an individual's malefic karma and purify/cleanse the individual. Each Malefic planet gets its turn during its Dasa or Antardasha to act on an individual's karma and produce results based on them. Every individual will have some good karma and some bad karma. The malefic planet will start analyzing from bad karma and in order to transform the individual will start working on those karmas based on its domain. For every negative karma in its responsible area it will go to any extent (including pursuing the individual from emotional to physical to psychic level) to make the individual suffer and realize that negative karmas will only yield negative results. Until the individual transforms, changes itself to produce benefic results the planet will follow itself to any plane and there will be no place to hide from its wrath. More negative the karma, more severe will be the results.

On the other hand, more the good karmas lesser will be the suffering. The svadharma of the malefic planets are harshness or punishment, however they have such nature so that they can maintain the balance of nature and the law of karma.

The benefic planets on the other hand comes with a gentle nature and will act on the positive karmas of the individual and based on those karmas will yield positive results.

Now why we discuss about the planets, astrology, karma and rebirth is another secret connected by a thin rope of occult study in an attempt to find some answers related to moksha or liberation.

Astrology is the branch of science that studies the universal forces acting on an individual since its inception in this material universe based on his/her karma and determines the path of his evolution or transformational process.

The individual will take birth only when the divine entities form the perfect configuration that indicates his karmic nature, nature of his soul and the direction in which his life cycle will travel farther. The time of his birth will be pre-determined by this universe and he/she is subject to the laws of this universe.

Now how the individual ascends to the mother's womb and from which **lok/layer** is a different discussion and we will address it later on this chapter.

What we need to understand here is that the area of unknown is infinite, and the area of our known world is finite. Although we have satellites, telescopes, and different biological instruments to study the nature of astral and biological life, however those instruments can only observe the physical realm and will not be able to penetrate into the spiritual realm of the entities. Every divine entity is alive whether it is Sun, the stars and the planets whether science agrees or not.

We need to stop here and ask ourselves few questions before we move ahead in this discourse.

- Are we thinking in the right direction? What is the relationship between a star and us if they are alive?

- If I understand transformation, what does it mean to be alive?

- If I am alive what is next? What should be my next plan of action to realize the way in which this universe wants me to operate?
- What if I do not believe in birth and death and I believe I have this life only to do whatever I want?

The above are valid questions that comes to each individual's mind who give some time to think about this life and what will happen the next. Other's simply does not have time or they are not bothered. They would like to act on what life offers and learns from them. They are definitely not smart thinkers and does not want to realize what the universe offers them in exchange of a human life. They are certainly not interested in this great opportunity and the divinity that the human life can offer them. They learn in course of time as they are working through the path of **karma Yoga.** Our path is a bit different; we will act through the path of **Bhakti Yoga** and universe will show us the way in which we can gain the knowledge of ultimate realization and understand this universal system and its components.

In this process, we submit ourselves to this vast universe and start floating in the direction in which it carries us. I was often remembering the movie **Life of Pie** while I was writing this chapter. Writing this chapter was never easy for me as I migrated from **India** to **Silicon Valley, California** with of course more Engineering work and it was the vast universe, which gave me direction and the strength to understand the true potential and power of this human life and the path of spiritual transformation.

Therefore, I would like to answer the above questions to the common readers, and it is up to them to conclude their understanding while we move ahead in this journey of transformation.

Answers:

- Definitely, we are thinking in the right direction. Stars are alive.

  My first chapter tells you how stars are born. You have also come to know that stars die, or they fall. When stars die, black holes are born which engulfs everything around them, space and time changes dramatically in them. Both science and mythology have enough evidence in them to prove these facts. The stars are what gives us life. Without sunlight, there can be no photosynthesis and hence no trees or human life is possible. That is why we Hindus worship Sun as god. **Suryanarayana** to us is Narayana manifesting in our daily life. I have already explained the concept of **Narayana** before. Hence, sun is from where every life begins and ends in this solar system. He is our true father and giver of life. Thus, the **father son** relationship exists between a star and us.

- To be alive simply does mean so many of things. In fact, to be alive means to think and act in multiple directions without any boundaries or limit. However, the most effective way would be towards a constructive process where our actions add to the growth of this universe and its benefic effects. We all have a profession. Living simply does not mean to be the best in our profession. Even butchers have a profession. The best butcher is certainly not the best of the individuals. An architect also has a profession.

The best architect can definitely build a beautiful monument/building, which several people can appreciate. Such an architecture adds to the growth of this universe. The doctor who treats the wounded of the earthquake victims is definitely contributing more to this universe as he is helping in the sustenance of life. Hence, Indians out of respect considers this noble profession as an act of godliness. Therefore, to be alive means we chose right profession, right way for the growth of the humanity. The process of universal transformation helps us to transcend inner growth and develop divine qualities that leads to the sustenance and growth of this universe. This process is lengthy and goes through several life cycles until our karma evolves through this spiritual journey to attain the abode of divine beings for higher karmic responsibilities. The universe helps in this process those who understand in this direction and are willing to attain the knowledge for directing the mind and action in the right path towards the higher responsibilities.

Thus, in this way an employee becomes CEO, an MP becomes Prime minister, and a **barrister** becomes a leader and Father of entire nation, a saintly **Mahatma Gandhi.** In modern age, I have never found a better example than **Swami Vivekananda** and **Mahatma Gandhi** who walked on this path of transcendence, transformation and attained divinity.

- The answer of this third question is elaborate and needs more clear explanation. Hence, I will answer it later on in this chapter when we discuss more on the process of inner transformation and the individual contribution to alter this universe.

- If I do not believe in birth, death, and that I have only this life to do whatever I want, then I should live my life as dew drops on lotus leaf, which will vanish and evaporate. This is what the Shastra's say. Live your life thinking it will evaporate. Live as if every moment is your last. When it ends, the person will be able to enjoy so much that he will feel he has attained heaven. This process of enjoyment will lead him to all the goodness, godliness and adventures that he will be unable to forget. There will be no desire left in his heart and he will never be born again. Nevertheless, this does not seem practical as whatsoever we do in a single life of 100 years with of course this physical body and limited thinking capability it is difficult to fulfill all of our wishes. Therefore, with of course a single unfulfilled wish we will also have the desire to fulfill that. Hence, with that single desire we will be born again to attain it, trapped in another cycle of infinite desires, which we can try to attain in single life. So, we will have to be born again with of course no choice whatsoever, whether we agree or not. This is how the nature works and we will always have to obey its laws whether we are alive or dead.

After we have answered the above questions, we move to the discussion of the lok/layer from which we descend onto this earth and the process of rebirth.

According to learned men, there are many planes above the physical plane where human beings transcend after their death. The astral plane is the one above this physical plane where we immediately ascend after this death and attain an astral body. We can attain astral body in dream if the mind and soul have already developed an astral consciousness. Based on karma human souls incarnate on the astral plane or they might degenerate to physical plane for purification. Thus, we descend into physical plane from astral plane.

From personal experiences, I can say that yes through dream in sleep we can achieve astral plane when we exist in our subtle bodies. I have experienced dreams, which often came true the next day in reality. Dream is the best astral vehicle to travel in astral plane if we develop the consciousness. Now we can find most of the answers of our questions from the Puranas and practitioners of divine consciousness.

Some of these answers we can find within ourselves through experiences, realization, and transformation. To develop an understanding, we need to gather information about the different worlds that exist around the place and us we ascend/descend during the process of transformation until we attain liberation.

This is a very simple concept similar to residing in India and yet to know about America. If we go there, someday this knowledge is definitely going to help us to exist. If we do not know about America it will simply does not mean that it really does not exist. It certainly exists and what is important is that we should know about it through our own thirst of knowledge so that we can experience the wonderful journey of traveling and existing in a completely different world.

Now going back to our discussion of planes/lokas/layers of

existence, according to esoteric astrology there are seven different layers of existence. They have different names according to different traditions and I have listed them in the below tabular format.

Theosophy	Various Eastern Designations				Translation
Monadic	Mahaparanirvana	Atala	Satyaloka	Adi	First
Divine	Paranirvana	Vitala	Taparloka	Anupadaka	Parentless
Spiritual	Nirvana	Sutala	Janarloka	Atma	Spirit
Unity		Rasatala	Maharloka	Buddhi	Intuition
Mental	Formless Heavens / Form Heavens	Taltala	Svarloka	Manas	Mind
Emotional	Desire Heavens	Mahatala	Bhuvarloka	Kama	Desire
Physical		Patala	Bhurloka	Sthula	Coarse

The famous Hindu Gayatri mantra speaks of these different layers that starts from the Bhur Lok and goes up to the Satya Lok. For the highest union with the creator of this universe the soul passes through these layers until it reaches Satya Lok.

The Vaishnava's call this layer Vaikuntha, the Shaiva's call this layer Shiva Lok, thus different worshippers of different forms of energy knows about this layer and have it different names according to the form they worship. Thus, the world where we reside is the one, which we perceive through our physical senses. Beyond these worlds, there are other worlds, which are subtle and exists in energy form. The most common of them is the astral layer, which is immediately above this layer, can be attained during sleep when our soul leaves our body and exists in subtle form. These out of body experiences help us further understand the subtle layers and energy forms that have existed in the past, existing in present and will be existing in future.

Time is a dimension in this physical world and has constraints. The yogis in the past has the power to do time travel based on out of body experiences, the subtle lokas where time is not a constraint and can be traveled to visualize the future.

Now Let us try to understand the layers of this universe in order to move to the next level in our attempt to realize the divine knowledge. This universe is composed of hidden dimensions and unseen realities that extends beyond the physical realities. Physicists call these dark matters and dark energy. In order to understand this divine knowledge, we must look to ancient Vedic /Puranas and alternative science and astrology.

As I mentioned before the universe is composed of seven layers of existence. Each of these layers are again composed of seven different sublayers, which makes this universe a forty-nine, fold existence model. The higher layers express more of energy aspect and hence are subtler. The lower layers express more of matter/physical aspect and hence are more material. These planes/layers are no specific locations; they all interpenetrate each other and occupy the same space. Based on different layers of consciousness developed we occupy these different layers.

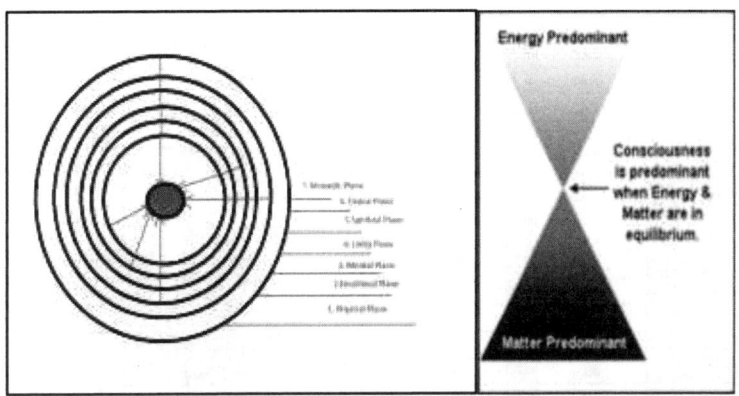

The energy aspect predominates on the upper layers i.e. on the monadic planes and the matter aspect predominates on the lower planes i.e. towards the physical planes.

On the denser physical planes, material aspects heavily restrict consciousness. The Tamas spreads like a serpent along the Sattva and Rajas gunas as dullness and ignorance of Tamas predominates over harmony, purity and wisdom. Its only through Rajas, the energy of transformation consciousness can be liberated to Sattva to attain these higher layers. As consciousness progresses up through the higher layers the material aspects decrease and the increasing energy aspects super charges the consciousness thus slowly it takes refuge in the monadic layers in the form of subtle energy.

Thus, these layers/planes are the cosmic planes of this universe and the lowest cosmic physical layer or our solar layer is composed of seven different sub layers, which are in the order of the diagram given above. Below is the complete diagrammatic representation.

43

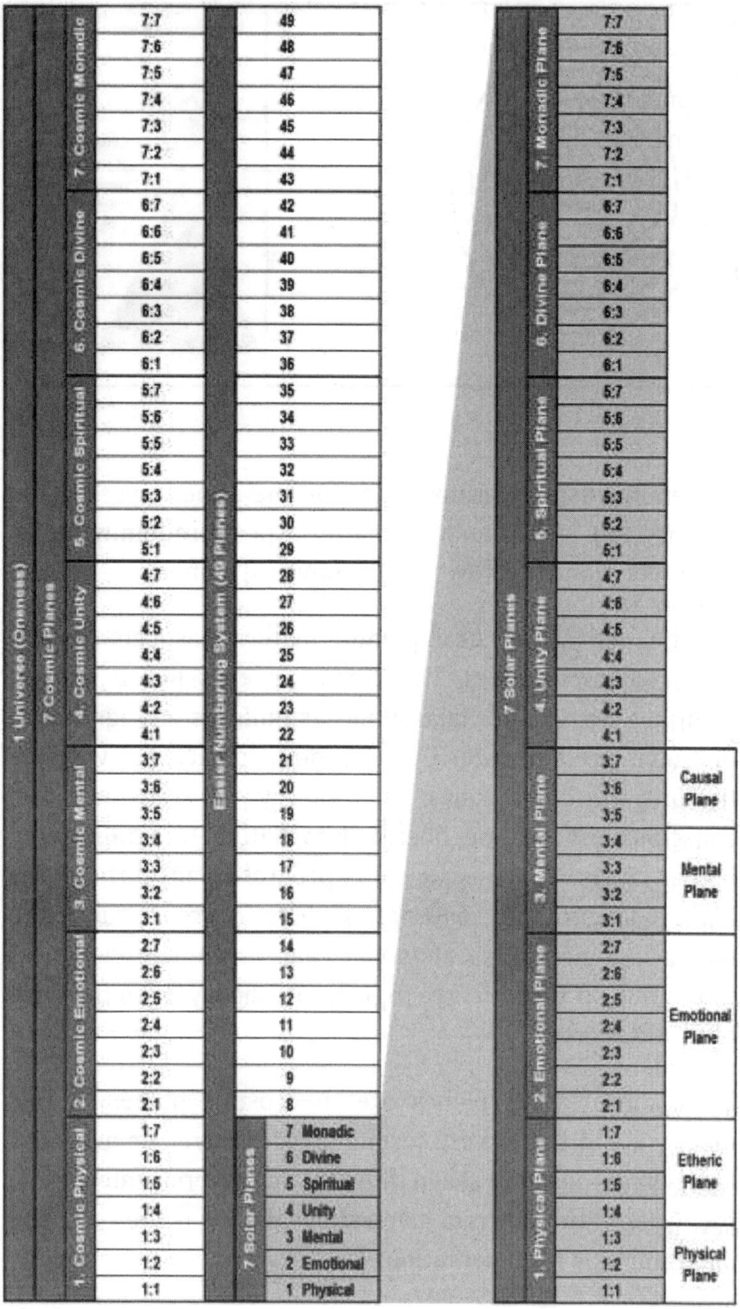

1 Universe (Oneness)
7 Cosmic Planes
Easier Numbering System (49 Planes)
7 Solar Planes

Cosmic Planes	Cosmic notation	Number	Solar notation	Solar / Right-most Planes
7. Cosmic Monadic	7:7	49	7:7	7. Monadic Plane
	7:6	48	7:6	
	7:5	47	7:5	
	7:4	46	7:4	
	7:3	45	7:3	
	7:2	44	7:2	
	7:1	43	7:1	
6. Cosmic Divine	6:7	42	6:7	6. Divine Plane
	6:6	41	6:6	
	6:5	40	6:5	
	6:4	39	6:4	
	6:3	38	6:3	
	6:2	37	6:2	
	6:1	36	6:1	
5. Cosmic Spiritual	5:7	35	5:7	5. Spiritual Plane
	5:6	34	5:6	
	5:5	33	5:5	
	5:4	32	5:4	
	5:3	31	5:3	
	5:2	30	5:2	
	5:1	29	5:1	
4. Cosmic Unity	4:7	28	4:7	4. Unity Plane
	4:6	27	4:6	
	4:5	26	4:5	
	4:4	25	4:4	
	4:3	24	4:3	
	4:2	23	4:2	
	4:1	22	4:1	
3. Cosmic Mental	3:7	21	3:7	3. Mental Plane — Causal Plane
	3:6	20	3:6	Causal Plane
	3:5	19	3:5	
	3:4	18	3:4	Mental Plane
	3:3	17	3:3	
	3:2	16	3:2	
	3:1	15	3:1	
2. Cosmic Emotional	2:7	14	2:7	2. Emotional Plane
	2:6	13	2:6	
	2:5	12	2:5	Emotional Plane
	2:4	11	2:4	
	2:3	10	2:3	
	2:2	9	2:2	
	2:1	8	2:1	
1. Cosmic Physical	1:7	7 Monadic	1:7	1. Physical Plane — Etheric Plane
	1:6	6 Divine	1:6	Etheric Plane
	1:5	5 Spiritual	1:5	
	1:4	4 Unity	1:4	
	1:3	3 Mental	1:3	Physical Plane
	1:2	2 Emotional	1:2	
	1:1	1 Physical	1:1	

(Lower number column label: 7 Solar Planes)

Now the time has finally come to explain the theory of reincarnation and some other interesting facts. The duality or transition of spirit and the theory of reincarnation rotate around two chief principles

- Death is impermanent and the monad (spirit/causal body) is the only permanent witness of all the experiences and memories that occurs during each incarnation.
- Only the enlightened beings descend with only one greater causal body (soul). For the others the causal body divides into two parts the greater and the lesser causal bodies (soul essence). This lesser causal body descends in this world.

Thus, the lesser causal body is essentially the replica of the greater causal body (soul) and descends into this physical plane with limited memory, knowledge and abilities to access the actual storehouse of memories, knowledge and abilities gathered in the greater causal body (soul) through the conscious mind. The soul or the greater causal body is the actual storehouse of our experiences in the human kingdom and contains the memories of all our human incarnations. Non-enlightened people fall asleep at some point during their ascent back to their soul and wake up at the same point as they descend into a new incarnation.

After each incarnation, the subtle bodies of our persona dissolve in sequence over the course of many years so the pathways to their memories are lost to us. New subtle bodies form for each new incarnation but they have no connection with our previous lives, so essentially, we are a new persona in each lifetime. The below table illustrates the memory retention methodology during the incarnation process.

45

	Primitive (monad in 1:7)	Civilised (monad in 2:7)	Developed (monad in 2:7)	Humanistic (monad in 3:4)	Enlightened (monad in 3:7)
Causal World	Unconscious	Unconscious	Unconscious	Semi-conscious	Conscious
Mental World	Unconscious	Semi-conscious	Semi-conscious	Conscious	Conscious
Emotional World	Semi-conscious	Conscious	Conscious	Conscious	Conscious
Physical-Etheric World	Conscious	Conscious	Conscious	Conscious	Conscious

Thus, it is the level of consciousness that defines the incarnation and the subtle bodies that it will form. For example, if as a human being someone has only enjoyed the art of taking without any action directed towards giving, then the consciousness is likely to be developed of a parasite that feeds on others and is dependent for its living on others generated resources only. It will also forget & loose its ability to generate resources for others. Hence, in the next incarnation it is likely to take the form of a parasite like mosquito or leech that feeds on the life energy of other creatures and has only the procreation ability to create parasites like themselves that can only feed but cannot feed others.

Incarnation as a human being is to take a physical form that can create a society, a human religion so unique that can think, act and align themselves for a better universe rather than limiting themselves on the basic plane of necessities. Human consciousness is a degenerated replica of the universal consciousness (Paramatma/God) in the physical plane. The sooner we realize this and align our karma for universal evolution the better will be our transformation towards achieving the divine plane and the subsequent process of transformation from reincarnation towards Moksha or Liberation from it.

As we know, Mother Earth or Mother Nature is a divine

entity in this universe and all the creatures that inhabit this planet are its children. Repeatedly we forget this truth and cause plight and pain to this planet by our destructive activities. This is the clue to a very important question that why the divine does incarnate time and often on this planet. When the plight of the nature becomes unbearable, she sheds its tears that are visible to the lord of the time, Lord Vishnu who is also the preserver of this creation.

In order to save his prakriti which is in the form of our mother nature he incarnates on this planet as a savior, a messiah to remind us of the path to the perfection and teach us the ideal life style through which we can contribute to the positive evolution of this universe and attain peace. Thus, the solution to end the man-made calamities like terrorism, animal slaughtering and racial violence lies in learning the cosmic knowledge and realizing the truth and transform into better human beings. It is important that we incorporate the divine qualities of forgiveness, truthfulness and non-violence in order to make this world a better place to live and die.

It is also important to understand that we are the portion of a body of the eternal vishwaroopam. If we hurt or harm the other parts of the same body of the vishwaroopam or system, we cause a great pain to our own body/system, which can lead to a spiritual disease so viral that the universal balance can disintegrate.

Thus, the vishwaroopam will not have any other choice rather than dissolving or annihilating the diseased part to create a new one to regain the balance incase if the disease of the part is untreatable and he is unable to heal it.

4. Shakti or Energy

Shakti or Energy is the driving force of this universe and the universes beyond this unknown & infinite universe. The reason I have chosen to write on this topic is that without understanding Shakti it is not possible to understand the divine energy principle, harvest its utilities for the betterment of the human society, and nurture its different components.

Definitely, I am not an expert in this field however; I have tried to collect the information from relevant sources in order to fulfill my quest in understanding the secrets of the nature and revealing the knowledge in simple and easy format to my target audiences who can later decide how to make use of it.

As a first step towards learning the divine energy, we will go through the process of understanding our mother nature and realize our true potential as human beings. The reason we fail often in our quests is that, we are casual in fulfilling our responsibilities towards the mother earth/nature. Our mortal body is made of flesh and blood, muscles and bones, which are completely biochemical components derived from mother earth itself. She has provided natural vegetation to provide nourishment to us. We tread on this earth and due to our greedy desires; we torment the other creatures who are also her children. We kill them, burn them for filling our stomach and support this savage act through our intellectual and smart brain. Human law does not punish a butcher and does not consider killing an animal a crime. Killing a human being is a crime as human life is precious; however, the life of an animal whom we slaughter is not precious to us. We justify our wrong act by saying that if we do not kill them for food, they will kill themselves for lack of space and resources. We ourselves increase the production of animals through artificial means in order to meet the rising demands. We kill them for our pleasure and greed and justify this act of cruelty through the sheer hypocrisy of human intelligence. Human beings can go to any extent in order to keep his mortal body alive. It is up to us to choose the path of being a non vegetarian and in that process karmically get associated to our food which is essentially another living creature in the food chain. This will leave behind a Karmic footprint of the creature who has sacrificed its life on us in the form of another Karmic debt known as the debt of the food to nature. We can also choose to be a Saint like **Prahlad Jani** to reduce our Karmic debts. **Prahalad Jani** as we all know have lived without food from 1940 due to the blessings of the divine mother. We can be intelligent in designing human laws and kill animals without caring for their pain or sufferings. However, to the divine mother all her children are equal and however smart we are, we are unable to escape her laws. Human beings can feel powerful temporarily by eating animals and fulfill his need for protein and fat, however the imbalance between the gunas in his body soon reduces his life span. Due to the Karmic debt mentioned before caused by the Tantra of food chain human beings feeding on another creature absorbs their energy including the energy of their diseases & also the energy of their pain and pleasure. Thus those who consumes meat their fate is sealed to suffer those diseases as that of their prey and often this may lead them to experience unknown fear which their prey felt when they suffered from the fear of slaughtering. If they don't suffer from this fear then probably they will suffer from a chronic heart disease if their consciousness probably doesn't awaken to let them understand the law of Karma. This is quite common nowadays. This is the judgement of nature and it is impartial and true. When men lie on deathbed and wonders why a chronic disease happened and eventually suffers and dies. He realizes diseases are nature's answers to human Karma in past/present life in order to make him feel helpless and realize his limitation and transforms him. If the above dawn of realization does not come to his intellectual mind and he is not "able to invoke his conscience" for sinful acts, nature gives him another sinful life to live and realize the truth behind his sufferings.

We tread on this earth, yet we destroy its natural resources. We call cow our mother because of the milk and love she provides to us, yet we cannot prevent cow butcher. These are the dark sides of our society. Our society is continuously degenerating & walking towards a calamity. Our main context here is how we lost our Shakti that had been once the glory of ancient India. The Shakti that has been our pride and is still present in textual form like Vedas, Bhagwat Gita, Ramayana, Jaimini & Parasara Astrology.

We need to stop here for some time and ponder where did we lost our soul and our Shakti. How can we revive the Shakti that operates at the level of enlightenment, spiritual bliss & eternal happiness? An energy that we can harness to produce positive results of healing our mind, body and attain peace, prosperity and health.

Well the answer seems within reach; however, in reality, it is still far off. In order to awaken and utilize such energy we have to use our psychic abilities, believe in our inner and spiritual self and experiment with infinity without any fear of annihilation or uncertainties. Our ancestors used to experiment with infinity, connect with the cosmic energies and use their psychic powers to harvest it within so that the eternal time can manifest the truth through their existence.

The world that we exist in is an illusion (Maya); the physical realities that manifest with time are created with the help of material energies that are responsible for awakening our consciousness within. Hence, we need to look beyond the physical realities and identify the subtle immaterial truth which is visualized when our third eye or the intuition chakra awakens. Intuition is a psychic power and a gift of God given to all those personalities whose past/present incarnation have an awakened third eye chakra due to accumulation of psychic abilities and Karma of penance, persistence and search for eternal truth. Some call it gut feeling, some guess and experts call it intuition, which differentiates a Yogi from a common person. Thus, intuition is a gift given by Mother Nature or Goddess Maya as a reward of purvapoonya. Goddess Maya or Prakriti is the physical manifestation of Purusha or Paramatma who is the *actual truth* & who is beyond all truths. The eternal pervasive infinity (Brahman) beyond space, time and above all realities is the eternal reality and only an enlightened being with an open third eye chakra can feel its presence.

I sincerely believe that every human being in this world have one or more psychic powers and everyone has some special gift within to transform someone's life and create an everlasting impact on the other individual. We call this process **Creative Mutation**. Thus, we can psychically influence and mutate this universe. The change can be positive or negative depending upon the nature of influence and the influencing entity/individual. Thus, a mutation can

51

be **Creative** or **Destructive** depending upon the above change. With mutation comes the evolution of a species. A **Creative Mutation** is often a response to a problem. It is as if a particular problem produced a form of life, which was appropriate to it. Thus, human beings are results of **Creative Mutation,** which is often a form of **cultural evolution** or **innovation**. Destructive Mutation can give rise to species/entities like asuras, which exists in layers called Patala.

I will hereby explain the process and the model by which we can invoke the Shakti and use it to perform **Creative Mutation** through which we can systematically transform the universal system into a spiritually evolving entity. This is essential to prevent complete annihilation of the human society during the **judgement day** or **Pralaya.**

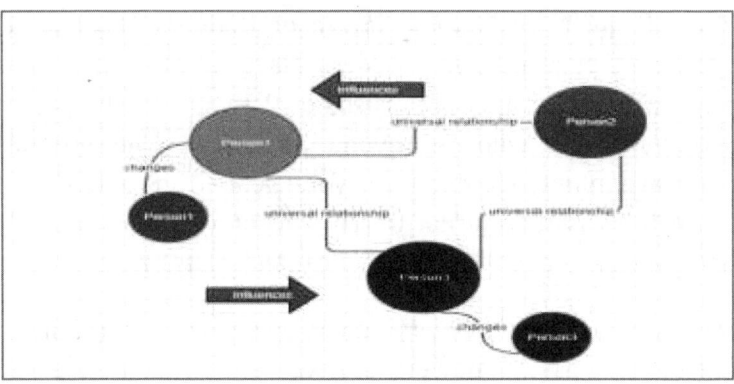

The diagram above considers a universal system of three entities; let us consider this system as an isolated system. This means that there is no external influence on this system and the energy of such an isolated system is constant.

In this system if an entity if capable of influencing another entity produces an effect of mutation where the entropy of the whole system changes towards thermodynamic equilibrium. Because of this mutation if we assume that person2 influences person1 and produces a change in him, person1 also can in turn influence person3 and changes its state. Person3 can also influence person2 and changes its state.

Thus, this is an interconnected system where each entity can influence and change each other. If this change is productive the system moves towards equilibrium with a productive evolution. Otherwise, the energy of the system becomes self-destructive, the equilibrium is unattained, and ultimately the system destroys itself in order to move towards equilibrium.

Thus, it is obvious that in this world worst things can also happen to good people. However, in such difficult times, there is no easy way out and we have to keep faith in the universal soul or god and pray that we pass the test successfully. Turning into evil in order to cure evil is no real solution. Because in such cases an evil is replaced by another evil. We have to thing rationally and move this system towards positive evolution. The real evil is the degenerated form of every goodness. It is the antonym of forgiveness, love, compassion, peace & harmony.

Hence, if someone is influencing us irrationally which can produce a destructive change in us; we need to reevaluate ourselves and should not let the above human qualities die within us. If we do that, the evil wins and our real self, our inner god loses. In such times if we articulate to ourselves that, our goodness is our existence and modulate the negative influence to transform it into a positive response towards the most difficult evil/foe we start transforming him. The initial responses might not be encouraging, and we might mistake that we are losing to transform. However, if we never give up and keep on continuing, we transform the other entity through our goodness. The connected system moves towards creative mutation and we transform it towards positive evolution.

With will power, man can even move a mountain. This is exactly the story of Dashrath Majhi, the mountain man who single handedly cut down a mountain. His story is the triumph of goodness over evil. Similar motivation we can get from Mahatma Gandhi who transformed the tyrant British and won freedom for India. The saint is now a subject of research in America and the whole world.

After exploring creative mutation, we will now see how great personalities like **Lord Rama, Lord Krishna** has used this power to transform & liberate degenerated souls like **Ravana** & **Duryodhana**.

According to the epic Ramayana **Ravana** was the grandson of **Sage Pulastya** who is one of the Saptarishis or seven stars of the *Ursa Major* (constellation of the northern sky). Some people regard him as the greatest ruler of the Lanka. However, his spiritual journey throughout his life have been full of degenerated piousness. He was a practitioner of demonic culture, thinking and methodologies. Through these practices, he committed grave crimes of kidnapping someone else's wife, imprisoning the **Navagraha** who regulate the wheel of karma & misusing the boon given by **Lord Brahma**, the creator to spread chaos, deception & evil into this world. Thus, it was important to transform this degenerated soul so that it can attain peace and liberation. As we have just seen in the last chapter, death is not the end of the spiritual journey. It is simply a transformation. Hence it is important that the soul learns its lesson before it leaves this body so that it can attain Moksha. In his previous birth, he was *Jaya* the gatekeeper of Vaikuntha and he was cursed. Hence, Lord Vishnu incarnated as Lord Rama to liberate the cursed soul. So Ravana was rather not killed by Rama in battle, he was liberated from his cursed life. The evil that Ravana spread was the result of the curse to disturb the balance of nature so that Vishnu the preserver of universe can incarnate and liberate him from his degenerated birth.

Now we will discuss about **Duryodhana** the greatest villain of the epic **Mahabharata** and how he attained Heaven after his demise in the battle of Kurukshetra. In the **Mahaprasthan Parva** of the Mahabharata it is said that when **Yudhishthira** entered heaven in his physical form, he saw Duryodhana sitting on a golden throne and smiling at him. Yudhishthira had previously seen other Pandavas suffering in the **Naraka**. He was surprised and asked Lord **Indra** that how was it that Duryodhana was enjoying the bliss of the Heaven whereas the rest of the Pandavas were suffering in the **Naraka**. Lord Indra then answered to Yudhishthira and said since Duryodhana perished in **Dharmayuddha** and died in Kurukshetra which was a blessed land he attained Heaven. This is a symbolic story which means that if a person dies in a conflict between Dharma and Adharma be it that the person had been on the wrong side of the conflict still he can attain heaven if the Lord Vishnu decides to liberate him out of his cursed life. His time and place of death will be set by the Lord Vishnu in such a way so that the Jivatmas gets liberated from their cursed life and attains the peace of heaven. The process of transformation happens during the conflicts of **Dharma** vs **Adharma** and the Jivatmas through their suffering transforms and gets liberated by the Lord from the curses incurred on them in their past lives.

These stories give hope to the common man that great sinners through eventual sufferings and transformations can be liberated by the Lord as and when through his will.

Now we will discuss & understand about **shakti** in more detail. **Robert J Oppenheimer**, the father of the atomic bomb was observing the Trinity test in New Mexico & immediately after the detonation of the first bomb said that he was observing the dance of **shakti**. As he witnessed the first detonation of a nuclear weapon on **July 16, 1945**, a piece of Hindu scripture ran through the mind of Robert Oppenheimer: "**Now I am become Death, the destroyer of worlds**". It is, perhaps, the most well-known line from the **Bhagavad-Gita**, but also the most misunderstood. Later, as two nuclear bombs were dropped on Hiroshima & Nagasaki in Japan the second world war ended. Oppenheimer's deep philosophy was just a glimpse of the vision he got when he truly understood the truth behind the scriptures of **Bhagavad-Gita.** This universe is a play of energies and we call this the **Rasleela** of the supreme Lord **Shri Krishna**. We get an idea of what a **Shakti** is capable of. **Shakti** can bring death & destruction and at the same time can end all conflicts and restore peace by ending the most devastating wars. It is the play of coming to an end & the start of new beginning. So, we as **Indians** we worship **Shakti**, after realizing the great potential of it and its driving power in this physical universe. Even though we cannot see the **Shakti** we know & understand its different forms and we have learned to respect it through ages of our accumulated ancestral knowledge. Cosmic Knowledge is the purest form of **Shakti**. Cosmic Knowledge about oneself not only does help in realizing the highest potential of a human being but also identifies the capabilities or **Shakti** hidden underneath oneself. **Identification** is the first step in the process and **Unlocking** it is the second step in the process. Once a human being can identify his shakti and unlocks it, the shakti can be used for the welfare of the human society and the universe. If required, this shakti can be transformed & used as the most devastating weapon the world has ever seen.

As I have previously given the example of the nuclear bomb which fits into this classical example. The scientists understood the highest potential of a nuclear fusion and converted the **shakti** into nuclear bomb. Since **Oppenheimer** was one of its creators, he realized both the devastating as well as the true **concluding** nature of the nuclear fusions. We everyday worship Lord Sun for the light he is giving to this world. Nevertheless, very few of us are aware of the nuclear fusion at its core as the source of this tremendous power or **Shakti**. A scientist is a human being who learns from the techniques of the nature through his observation. So essentially a scientist converts the spiritual power of this universe into physical realities and leverages it. So, **Thomas Alva Edison** using the same Shakti Principle leveraged the thunder power of electricity to lighten up the world & **Robert J Oppenheimer** to summon the **Brahmashir Astra** or the modern nuclear bomb.

Oppenheimer knew that the great war would eventually end many human lives, but he realized that the great Lord has chosen him as a medium to end this war.

As he understood the true potential of the **Nishkam Karma** in the Gita, where Lord Shri **Krishna** preaches **Arjuna** to fight the battle of **Dharma** and remain detached from the consequences. He tells Arjuna that his duty is to fight, and he has the right only to fight; he does not have any control on the outcome. So, the great truth came upon **Oppenheimer** and it saved him from the guilt of the devastating effects of the bombs on the two **Japanese** cities. He understood that he was in the shoes of **Arjuna** and he had to do what is necessary his duty. It is here where he submitted his karma unto Shri **Krishna** and let him decide the fruits of it. So, history doesn't remember him necessarily as a person who was responsible for the destruction of the **Japanese** but rather as the father of the modern nuclear bomb. However, history does remember **Hitler** as the cause of the second world war & the blood bathed history of the **Nazis**. Even though Hitler adopted the great **Swastika** icon of the **Hinduism** as a symbol of Nazi flag it could not liberate him. In doing so his primary reason was, he attached himself to the fruits of Karma. He was aware that **Swastika** symbolized **"good fortune"** and he wanted the support of it for all his acts. He indeed got the support of it and recorded his name in the history but for all the wrong reasons. His attachment to the fruits of Karma kept him away for the sole purpose of it and he did not understand the right essence of **Bhagavad-Geeta** which **Oppenheimer** did. In attaching himself to the fruits of Karma **Hitler** distanced himself from the Lord just like **Suyodhana** and at the end of the war met the same fate as **Duryodhana**. He might today be sitting in heaven and smiling back at me as I write this book as he was also one of the mediums chosen by the **Lord** for his Leela in this world to make us understand the dance of shakti.

When a human being understands its true potential, he can transform himself to embrace the grace of the god. The science of Yoga is designed to prepare the aspirant physically and spiritually and at the end this Yogi realizes his Shakti in its purest form. The classic example of it is **Shri Guru Gobind Singh Ji** who used his Yogic power to transform the Sikhs into a martial race. The rest is history where Sikhs stands to protect the common men against the atrocities & cruelty of the Mughal ruler **Aurangzeb**. **Martial art & Military** is based on same principle where one understands the Shakti deep rooted within and converts the mind and body into a weapon for supporting the defense system of one's nation or country. Similarly, the sportsmen use this martial art but at a controlled intensity and focus more at a **competitive & artistic** edge to achieve the end goals as per the rules of the game.

Now we will try to study on the human anatomy of the Shakti centers in the physical body & what are the astrological planets related with those energy centers. Given below is the diagram of the Seven upper Chakra System in the human body and each chakra corresponds to an upper astral consciousness in the human psychic system.

There are two tables given below which shows the relationship of each Chakra with the Astrological planetary systems & Psychic Astral bodies correspondingly.

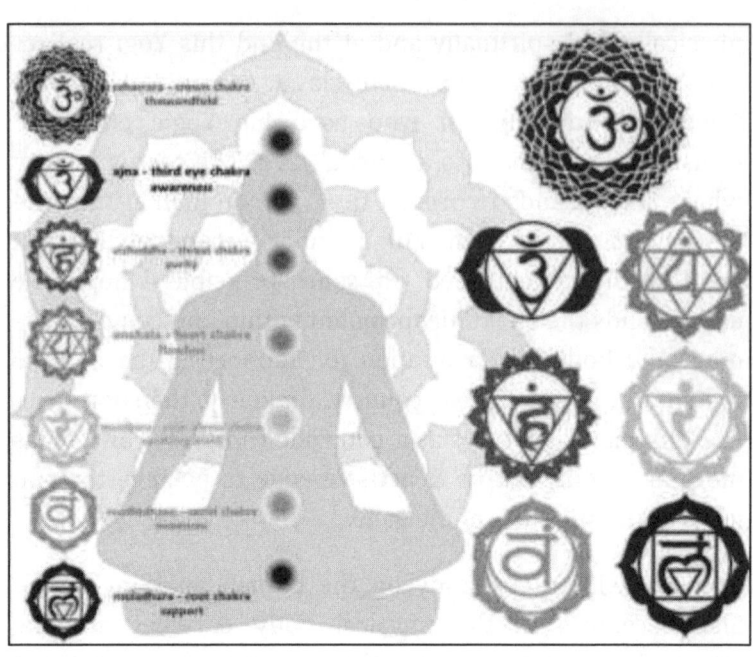

Chakra	Chakra Expression	Ruling Planet	Planetary Karaka
Seventh/Crown	I understand	Jupiter	Expansion, generosity, opening
Sixth/Third Eye	I see	Saturn	Limitation, time, inevitable consequences
Fifth/Throat	I speak	Mercury	Creativity, expression
Fourth/Heart	I love	Moon	Peacefulness, bliss, heartedness
Third/Solar Plexus	I do	Sun	Brightness, confidence, optimism

Second/ Sacral	I feel	Venus	Sensuality, tenderness, spontaneity
First/Root chakra	I am	Mars	Ability to survive, stability

Chakra	Color	Astral Body
Seventh/Crown	Violet	Nirvanic Body
Sixth/Third Eye	Deep Blue	Cosmic Body
Fifth/Throat	Turquoise	Spiritual Body
Fourth/Heart	Green	Mental Body
Third/Solar Plexus	Yellow	Astral Body
Second/ Sacral	Orange	Etheric Body
First/Root	Red	Physical Body

Each of the above Astral bodies operate at the subtle Astral planes of existence already discussed in the previous chapter. So, the anatomy of our inner psychic system is a layered concentric structure like an onion. Inner exploration penetrates each layer and reaches the innermost core of the Brahman situated in us.

Now that we have discussed the seven Chakra System and the astral bodies corresponding to each the immediate question that comes to our mind is how we activate these chakras and what are the capabilities we have for activating them.

The answer lies in a deep coiled form of **Shakti** located at the base of the spine and in the first chakra known as **Kundalini**. It is depicted as a sleeping coiled snake which when awakened can start moving up or down. As this primordial cosmic energy penetrates each Chakra and moves up gradually it activates each one of them. In this process the corresponding astral bodies are also awakened, and the individual can transcend in the higher planes of existence through the awakened consciousness of the Chakras. Through the astral bodies corresponding to each Chakra the yogis can travel through the higher planes of existence while keeping their physical body in the physical plane of existence. If we are born as a human being therefore our sole purpose should be to awaken the Kundalini Shakti so that we can attain the higher layers of Consciousness and participate in the process of evolution.

Otherwise the conditioned **Jivatmas** sleeping Kundalini remains in coiled state at the Root Chakra and the individual gets stuck in eternal infinite cycles of birth & death and his "Ego" consciousness never allows him to rise above earthly survival, miseries & struggles of physical plane existence. Therefore, wise men transcend for becoming Yogis and rise above religious practices and rituals of a particular religion, caste or society through their scientific spiritual research and contribute as a reformer. Therefore, it is advisable to try and become a Yogi in order to attend Liberation. Yogis can travel the dimensions of space and time without any restriction and gets the privilege by the grace of Lord Shri Krishna to work through the cycles of Birth & Death willingly.

Now how do we track & predict if a person born among us has yogic capabilities or not. The answer is very simple, we need to study the astrological charts in order to understand the planetary positions, their strengths & the birth nakshatra. By the will of the Lord time operates on this universe and by his will alone all conditioned souls take birth in this physical plane of existence. Astrology is rightly said as the **"Eyes of the Vedas"**. We therefore through astrology can understand the purpose for which the conditioned soul has taken birth, the direction of various aspects of their life & the journey that the conditioned soul will undertake to fulfill its purpose. We can also through astrology understand which plane of existence the soul was resting earlier before taking its birth. Thus, astrology offers a wide variance of techniques to understand about the psychic forces acting on a human being. A good astrologer will have a very sound intuition & visual abilities as his third eye chakra would be highly energetic & active and using his third eye can communicate with the cosmic entities through astrology. A good astrologer is thus a messenger of Lord. A human being will only get interested to study astrology if he has been blessed by Lord. Thus, only a blessed human being will study astrology and only very few of them would be able to comprehend it through scientific methods by the blessings of almighty Lord. Very few among them would be able to understand, visualize and predict accurately. In this **Kalyuga** since very few Yogis are born, we are left with only limited options like Astrology to study the depths of cosmic truth. However, if we can continuously practice the principle of **Bhakti Yoga**, we will be able to work through the dark age of Kalyuga by the grace of the divine Lord. By his grace of kind Lord, we will have the abilities to transform our mortal nature to invoke our **Kundalini** shakti and work through the conditioned wear and tear of the physical existence to activate our Chakras. **Bhakti Yoga** itself has the power to invoke **Karma Yoga** and finally **Gyan Yoga** to

63

attain Moksha. We will discuss in detail about this topic in chapter 15 of this book. Thus, in this chapter we tried to understand how Shakti the primordial cosmic energy is in the base of creation & existence. It is the powerful cosmos in itself & is the agent of all changes & mutations. Sanatan Dharma worships Shakti as the universal mother & the form which enables the all-pervading **Brahman** to materialize & manifest itself.

Now we will discuss briefly about the concepts of **Shakti Peethas** as without mentioning them this chapter cannot be considered as complete.

The word **Shakti Peethas** means Chakra Centers of this earth. It is believed that there are 52 **Shakti Peethas** and each of them has a temple constructed to mark the significance of the place. It is said that after Lord **Vishnu** divided the material body of mother **Sati** the eternal consort of Lord **Shiva** into 52 pieces using his **Sudarshan Chakra** the beautiful wheel of time, they fell on different places on this earth. Mother Earth is another form of **Shakti** and the pieces thus did not fell randomly on earth. By the law of nature and the principle of electromagnetism, they fell only on the **Shakti** Centers of this earth as mother nature absorbed the eternal cosmic energy of the primordial shakti. Thus like 7 Chakras of the human psychic system there are 52 Chakras of the Mother Earth. We worship them and has constructed temples for pilgrimages so that by visiting these energy points we can activate those cosmic energies in our lives to realize the truth behind the physical manifestation of the all-pervading and formless **Brahman** in the form of Lord **Shiva**. The activation of these cosmic energies in our life ecosystem will thus bestow us with prosperity and peace.

It is said that **Shiva** Loka, the abode of Lord **Shiva** exists on the Mount **Kailash** in the Himalayas. If we carefully observe the structure of Mount Kailash, we will understand that it is the Crown Chakra or the Sahasrara of this earth. Thus, it is the abode of supreme consciousness or **Shiva** the ultimate truth on this earth. Thus, a Yogi who meditates after taking a bath in divine **Man Sarovar taal (Lake)** will be able to activate his crown Chakra by the grace of the divine Lord. He will be able to realize the ultimate truth or **Shiva** and get liberated from this endless bondage of births and deaths. He will be able to repay all his Karmic debts by the grace of the divine god through his bhakti and become a free unconditioned soul. **Shiva** is truth and the only cycle of truth is the cycle of destruction and recreation. Thus, **Shiva** or **Rudra** works over the dissolution of the material nature at the end of **Manvantaras** or the divine cycle of time.

It is believed that Mother **Sati** reincarnated as Mother **Parvati** the daughter of the mighty Himalayas. She reunited with Lord **Shiva** and their family resides in the Mount **Kailash**. Thus, metaphorically speaking the eternal cosmic truth **(Shiva)** and the eternal cosmic energy **(Shakti)** both united at Mount **Kailash**. Hence, it's the Crown Chakra of this earth too where the Kundalini Shakti of **Sati** from the 52 different **Shakti Peethas** unites with **Shiva** in the form of **Parvati** in the highest abode of the Himalayas. Now atheists who wants to argue might say that Mount **Everest (again located on the Himalayas)** is the highest peak of the world so why not it's the Crown Chakra of the earth. To them the answer would probably be that **Everest** is the height of the Himalayas his glory standing tall & **Kailash** his divine consciousness.

5. Brahma & The Brahman

The **Brahma Gayatri** mantra best describes Lord Brahma and is given below. The meaning of these hymns is given below correspondingly.

1. *Om Chathur mukhaya Vidmahe, Hamasaroodaya Dheemahe, Thanno Brahma Prachodayath*

    ➤ Let me meditate on the god with four faces, Oh God who rides on the swan, give me higher intellect, and let the Lord Brahma illuminate my mind.

2. *Om Vedathmanaya Vidmahe, Hiranya Garbhaya Dheemahi, Thanno Brahma prachodayath*

    ➤ Let me meditate on the god who is the soul of the Vedas, oh god who holds the entire world within you, give me higher intellect and let the Lord Brahma illuminate my mind.

The **Brahma Gayatri** mantra is self-explanatory & is the most authentic text on Lord Shri Brahma. These four lines of poetic texts in Sanskrit tells us everything we need to know about Lord Brahma for an introduction. He is the first Purusha, the first eternal celestial being of this universe born out of **Hiranyagarbha**. Hence, the universe is named after him as **Brahmanda,** which means the egg of Brahma. In the first chapter we have discussed the cosmic process by which the universe was born. In the modern science it has been proved that the universe is elliptical. Thus, the egg shaped, or elliptical universe is the base of all the physical plane of existence & at the core of this egg lies Lord Brahma in his abode known as Brahma Loka. **Brahma** is the creator of all the worlds (higher & lower than the **Martyaloka** or Abode of Human beings) within this universe. We have discussed about the various planes of existence in chapter 3 earlier.

Brahma's four heads signify four Vedas Rig, Sama, Yajur & Atharva. Anyone who is completely knowledgeable of the four Vedas are known as **Chaturvedi.** Thus, Lord Brahma is the first **Chaturvedi.** He is the source & creator of Vedic knowledge. His four heads also symbolize the three dimensions of space and the fourth dimension of time. His four heads also symbolize the four Yugas or Chathur Yugas-**Satya, Treta, Dwapar & Kali** of the Hindu Divine Cosmology.

His four heads are the four main **Varnas** or the caste system based on the type of profession a human pursues of this human society.

The four-fold main divisions into which the human society individuals can be classified based on professional identity are.

- **Brahmins-** Intellectuals & knowledge-based personnel like Professors, Scientists, Teachers, Priests, Poets, Writers, Diplomats etc.

- **Kshatriyas-** Political & Administrative, Military, Legal & Defense Expert personnel.

- **Vaishyas-** Farmers & Cultivators, Business & Corporate, Sales & Management, Artists, Architect personnel.

- **Shudras-** Labors & Service personnel.

Other professional identities are a complex combination of these four main Varnas.

The Hindu caste system is the most misunderstood caste system in the world. In the beginning the Varna system was followed based on individual professional identity as prescribed by the Vedas. Later with the degeneration of Vedic knowledge & society corruption this varna system got changed from merit based professional identity to family based professional identity. Due to Lack of administration of the Varna system from the Kings in the later vedic period, the essence of the Karmic varna based system based was lost. Merit was little considered for **Shudra** varnas and they were pressurized politically & diplomatically to pursue the same professional identity as their forefathers.

The **Shudras** were deprived of education & other benefits to make them pursue same work as their ancestors during the foreign rule of India. The Mughals and the British further exploits them for their own benefits and forcibly converted their religion by manipulation and used this manpower for their own agenda. Some of these people out of their fear escaped into the forests during subsequent foreign invasion & rule and became the forests dwellers. They were not accepted back into the mainstream society later due to their nomadic and unhygenic lifestyle thereafter. Thus the caste system became more complex. These poisonous practices slowly became society norms and the Varna system became the most misunderstood system in the world and thus began the dark age of the fall of the Vedic Knowledge.

In **Shrimad Bhagwat Purana** it has been mentioned in detail how Lord *Brahma* originated from **Param Brahma (Paramatma)** & the eternal **Brahman Garbhodakshayi**

Vishnu. Here we will have to understand that there are two different ways of understanding the eternal & all-pervading **Brahman or Paramatma** which transcends over all universal entities (living, non-living & dead). These two ways are known as **Dvaityavad** or **Advaityavad.** **Dvaityavad** means duality and it agrees that the eternal **Brahman** has both formless and formed nature. So **Dvaityavad** considers both the material & the energy form of the same cosmic entity & is a more practical approach. **Dvaityavad** also considers both the law of conservation of energy & that different forms of energy are interconvertible while their integration remains constant.

Advaityavad endorses non-dualism and focuses on only one aspect of the eternal **Brahman** & our unidirectional relationship to him only in the phase of complete dissolution of this universe. Both these ways of understanding are valid but their applicability to circumstances are unique.

Just as quantum mechanics agrees that light has both particle & wave nature, Hindu **Dvaityavad** too agrees on the same dual nature of the supreme soul or **Paramatma**. Thus, the supreme consciousness of the **Paramatma** is the eternal all-pervading **Brahman**. Thus, it is evident that the eternal **Brahman** exists in all universal entities as its formless consciousness.

Thus, the **Paramatma** is the soul/energy nature of the particle/material nature of the infinite Shri **Garbhodakshayi Vishnu &** the all-pervading **Brahman** is his supreme consciousness. Thus, Lord **Garbhodakshayi Vishnu** created **Lord Shri Brahma** & this universe which consists of 3-dimensional space, fourth dimension of time & seven dimensions of alternate realities. These seven alternate realities have been discussed in detail in Chapter 3 & the seven higher chakras corresponding to each of these alternate realities can be used to perceive them.

Thus, by whatever name we call **Brahman** or **Paramatma** or **Vishnu** they lead ultimately to the same Infinite **Shri Vishnu.** Since Hindu cosmology is very complex due to its scientific nature it is almost incomprehensible and confusing to our mortal & limited intellect. However, those who are persistent in their search of truth by the grace of Lord Shri **Vishnu** will be able to understand the scientific & true nature of this galactic cosmology.

After **Brahma** of this universe emerged from the sprouting consciousness of **Shri Vishnu** described as a lotus & trying to figure out the origin of his source, surprisingly he was unable to trace his roots. The helpless **Brahma** on the infinite cosmic ocean of this universe was left alone and his inability to comprehend his source & the reason of his birth left him in a deep state of introspection. **Brahma** thus in the quest of truth & to find the answers of his queries meditated upon the supreme infinite & his creator.

Thus, **Brahma** upon meditating for a very long time was able to develop the knowledge & the vision of the supreme Infinite. He saw the self-illuminated Shri **Vishnu** lying on the coiled Infinite **Sesh Naga** (Coiled Primordial Serpent Energy of the universe) upon the infinite cosmic ocean of the vast universe. Thus, the lord's magnificent infinite form was very difficult to comprehend & explain as it had no beginning & no end. However, as we understand **Brahma's** and **Arjuna's** experience was similar seeing the infinity in front of them. Thus, we as mortal human beings came to know of the infinite Shri **Vishnu** through the eyes of **Shri Brahma** &

Arjuna as described in the **Brahmanda Purana** & **Shrimad Bhagwat Purana.** His self-illuminated and infinite form is beyond any poetic or literary description & transcends over linguistic limitations. His true form is also beyond comprehension & any imagination. Any attempt to do so will evoke fear, uncertainty & can cause destabilization of the mind. Thus, **Brahma** after knowing the truest form of Shri **Krishna** surrendered unto his creator. Shri **Krishna** thus pleased by the Brahma enlightened him removing all his illusion & ignorance.

He thus granted his blessings to **Brahma** that he will be able to meditate & communicate with him whenever he wishes from deep inside his heart. Shri **Krishna** also said to **Brahma** that he will see the infinite consciousness of him in all the beings that he will create & all over the universe whenever Shri **Brahma** is free from all influences of the modes of material nature & that he will realize that he is the one form of the eternal **Brahman.** He thus entrusted **Brahma** with the cause of the creation of the worlds & the entities within them.

Upon receiving the orders of the supreme lord, the enlightened **Brahma** thus began the task of creation. However, **Brahma** had to face a bigger challenge before starting his job of creation. This challenge was in the form of two demons named **Madhu** & **Kaitabha.** These two demons originated from the earwax of the sleeping **Garbhodakshayi Vishnu. Garbhodakshayi Vishnu** was in a meditative deep sleep known as **Yoganidra.** These demons originated due to **Yoga Maya** which is **Vishnu's** induced alternate reality in the universe & is an integral part of it existing in the form of illusion. Thus, the sleeping **Garbhodakshayi Vishnu** wanted to send a bigger message to **Brahma** that the creator

Brahma himself needs protection & sustenance from greater evil while he is carrying out his job. Thus, **Madhu** & **Kaitabha** emerged out of Vishnu Leela (sport of **Yoga Maya/Mahamaya**) to teach him the same.

Madhu and **Kaitabha** performed a long period of tapas devoted to goddess Mahadevi. The goddess granted them the boons of invincibility and voluntary death. The proud-filled demons then started attacking **Brahma**. Brahma sought Vishnu's help but was unable to awaken Vishnu who was still in deep meditative sleep. **Garbhodakshayi Vishnu** then created his replica as **Ksirodakasayi Vishnu** who is the Paramatma, sustainer & protector of this universe.

The **Ksirodakasayi Vishnu** assured **Brahma of** protection & sustenance and fought against the demons. However, he was defeated by the two demons and he had to employ a trick to destroy the two demons.

Ksirodakasayi Vishnu praised the battle powers of the two demons and said that he was pleased to grant them boons. The boastful demons, proud of their victories against Vishnu, said that they were willing to grant him boons instead. **Vishnu** cleverly asked **Madhu** and **Kaitabha** for their lives and they were forced to kill each other. **Ksirodakasayi Vishnu** thus emerged even before Brahma started his creation as the protector & sustainer of this universe. **Garbhodakshayi Vishnu** knew that **Brahma** would need his active support to do his job. He thus used his **Yoga Maya** to create a Leela(sport) for making this adventurous and a challenging experience for **Brahma** in order to prepare him for the greater challenges in the future & also at the same time took this opportunity to create his replica at the single universe level.

Now we will discuss about the various creations of Lord **Brahma** & at the end about the concepts of four Yugas or divine cycles.

At the beginning Lord **Brahma** was a little bit confused since he was left with the vast possibilities of creation, he wondered about what about kind of creation he would create first. Finally, after much thinking he focused on creating symmetric forms.

Brahma at the beginning created four **Kumaras** (sages) out of his mind. They are known as his **manasputras**. These manasputras roamed the universe as kids and they were named **Sanaka** (ancient), **Sanatana** (eternal), **Sanandana** (ever joyful) & **Sanatkumara** (ever young). **Brahma** in desire of company created them and wanted to entrust them with the responsibilities of creation. However, they refused to procreate and instead chose celibacy and remained devoted to study. They are said to wander throughout the materialistic and spiritualistic universe without any desire but with the sole purpose to teach. **Brahma** angered at this disobedience frowned. Out of his anger from his forehead was born **Rudra**. This **Rudra** is known as Shiva the ultimate truth of the universe. This **Rudra** or the wrath of **Brahma** known as Shiva is associated with the task of the dissolution & destruction of the worlds as and when **Brahma** wishes for recreation. Thus, **Brahma**, **Vishnu** & **Shiva** are three different forms of the same eternal **Brahman**. So whatever form one wishes can meditate or worship upon one will associate to that aspect of the eternal **Brahman** by meditating on that form.

Now there is a very interesting fact associated with the **Kumaras** and how they were the prime factors responsible for the most famous incarnations of **Vishnu** like **Varaha, Narsimha, Rama & Krishna**. These four Kumaras, as siddhesvaras, had achieved all the yogic perfectional achievements (siddhis), and as such, they travel in outer space without machines. **Prithu** and sage **Narada** were fortunate to receive knowledge from these Kumaras. The abode of **Ksirodakasayi Vishnu** is known as **Vaikuntha**. Due to the boon from their father Brahma and the strength of their tapas, the Four Kumaras looked like 5-year-olds. **Jaya** and **Vijaya**, the gatekeepers of the **Vaikuntha** stopped the Kumaras at the gate, thinking them to be children. They told the Kumaras that Sri **Vishnu** is resting and that they cannot see him. The enraged Kumaras cursed both **Jaya** and **Vijaya** that they would have to give up their divinity, be born as mortals on Earth (**Bhuloka**).

This curse was eventually 'diluted' by **Vishnu** to **Jaya** and **Vijaya** choosing to be born three times on Earth as enemies of incarnations of **Vishnu** and that he would liberate them. Thus, **Vishnu** is always benevolent on his devotees and he thus to liberate them from curses of past lives takes various incarnations. Thus, **Jaya** and **Vijaya** incarnated as **Hiranyakashipu** and **Hiranyaksha** in Satya Yuga; **Ravana** and **Kumbhakarna** in Treta Yuga; finally, **Shishupala** and **Dantavakra** in Dvapara Yug.

Brahma in order for the cycle of creation to continue created ten more sons or **Manasputras Angira, Atri, Bhrigu, Daksha, Kratu, Marichi, Narad, Pulastya, Pulaha** and **Vashista** & one daughter or **Saraswathi**. **Brahma** was so much taken over by the illusion of the beauty of his own daughter that he began to pursue her. **Brahma** was so infatuated with her that he developed a fifth head of lust. **Rudra** or Shiva then chopped off the fifth head of **Brahma**

74

and cursed him that he will never be worshipped in this world. It's because of this reason that **Brahma** is not worshipped and there is only one temple of **Brahma** in Pushkar, India. **Brahma's** punishment came by way of him losing all his powers of penance, due to his desire for his daughter. Powerless to create, he had to appoint his sons to take forth the act of creation. **Brahma** was then free to 'own' **Saraswati**. She ran from him and assumed the female forms of many a creature; but **Brahma** was not to be spurned and followed her across the universe with the corresponding male forms of those creatures.

They were eventually 'married' and their union gave rise to all manner of species. He made love to her, and from their union the progenitors of mankind were born. **Brahma** and **Saraswati** became the Cosmic Couple. Apparently, the primordial man **Manu** was his son. **Manu** was married to **Shatarupa** & had two sons ,**Priyavarta & Uttanpad** and three daughters **Aakooti, Devhooti & Prasuti**. Aakooti was married to Ruchi Prajapati, Prasuti was married to Daksha and Devhooti was married to Kardam rishi. It is their children who went on and populated the Earth. **Brahma** also created such things as Dharma (righteousness or Truth) and Adharma (un-Truth), anger, desire, fear, attachment, joy, and suffering. **Brahma** also created various worlds and the celestial creatures inhabiting them such as **Gandharva, Yaksha, Kinnara, Kimpurusha, Rakshasa, Nagas, Suparna, Vanaras, Vidyadhara, Vasus, Pisacha, Devas, Danavas & Asuras**. We will briefly discuss about the ten **Manasputras** of Brahma below.

- **Marichi Rishi-** Rishi Marichi (meaning a ray of light) is also one of the **Saptarishis** (Seven Great Sages Rishi), in the First **Manvantara**, with others being

Atri Rishi, Angiras Rishi, Pulaha Rishi, Kratu Rishi, Pulastya Rishi, and Vashista. Marichi is married to Kala and gave birth to **Kashyap**.

- **Atri Rishi-** When the sons of Brahma were destroyed by a curse of Shiva, Atri was born again from the flames of a sacrifice performed by Brahma. His wife in both manifestations was **Anusuya**. She bore him three sons, Datta, Durvasa, and Soma, in his first life, and a son Aryaman (Nobility), and a daughter, Amala (Purity), in the second. Soma, Datta, and Durvasa are the incarnations of the Divine Trinity Brahma, Vishnu, and Rudra (Shiva) respectively.

- **Angirasa Rishi-** **Angirasa** is a rishi who, along with sage Atharvan, is credited to have formulated ("heard") most of the fourth Veda called Atharvaveda. He is also mentioned in the other three Vedas. His wife is Surupa and his sons are Utathya, Samvartana, and Brihaspati.

- **Pulaha Rishi-** He was born from the navel of Lord Brahma. He was burned due to a curse made by Lord Shiva, then was born again in **Vaivasvata** Manvantara, this time from Agni's hair.

- **Pulastya Rishi-** He was the medium through which some of the Puranas was communicated to man. He received the Vishnu Purana from Brahma and communicated it to Parasara, who made it known to mankind. He was one of the Saptarishis in the first Manvantara. He was the father of Visravas whose sons were Kubera and Ravana, and all the Rakshasas & Yaksha are supposed to have sprung from him.

Visravas had two wives: one was Kaikesi who gave birth to Ravana, Kumbhakarna, and Vibhishana; and another was Ilavida and had a son named Kubera who was a Yaksha and known as god of wealth.

- **Krathu Rishi-** Kratu which appears in two different ages. In the Swayanbhuva Manvantara. Krathu was a Prajapati and a very dear son of Lord Brahma. He was also the son-in-law of Prajapati Daksha. It is said that he had 60,000 children. They were named as **Valakhilyas** which signifies Hobbits of Indonesia or Pigmies of Africa.

- **Vashista-** He is one of the Saptarishis in the seventh, i.e. the present Manvantara. He had in his possession the divine cow Kamdhenu, Nandini who could grant anything to their owners. His wife is Arundhati Devi. In cosmology, Mizar star is known as Vashista and Alco star is known as Arundhati in traditional Indian astronomy. The pair is considered to symbolize marriage and, in some Hindu communities, priests conducting a wedding ceremony allude to or point out the constellation as a symbol of the closeness marriage brings to a couple.

- **Daksha-** Prajapati Daksha and his wife Prasuti had 24 daughters of which 13 were married to sage Kashyap and the one known as Sati married Shiva. Sati is known as Adi Shakti or the incarnation of primordial female energy.

- **Bhrigu-** Maharishi Bhrigu is the first compiler of predictive astrology, also the author of Bhrigu Samhita, the astrological classic. The adjectival form of the name, Bhargava, is used to refer to the descendants and the school of Bhrigu. Along with Manu, Bhrigu had made important contributions to 'Manu smriti', which was constituted out of a sermon to a congregation of saints in the state of Brahmavarta, after the great floods in this area, nearly 10,000 years ago. His daughter is Lakshmi and married **Vishnu**. One of his sons is the famous astrologer & guru of the Danavas Shukracharya whose abode is the planet Venus known to rule over human fertilization & potency.

- **Narada-** The eternal wanderer, messenger & ardent devotee of Lord Shri Vishnu.

Now the most important part of this chapter is a tale from **Mahabharata** which proves metaphorically that **Sanatan Dharma** Rishis knew & understood the concepts of relativity of time & also the existence of parallel universes almost 5000 years ago. Modern day scientists like **Einstein** discovered the theory of relativity & **Stephen Hawkins** talks about parallel universes, however **Mahabharata** states it in a beautiful narrative much way back than we can imagine.

The tale goes back to the time when Shri **Krishna** was on the earth at the beautiful **Vrindavan** & through his amazing childhood Leela was quenching the thirst of his devotees. One day, Lord **Brahma**, heard about Krishna. He also got to know that Krishna has recently killed a demon in the form of a huge python named **Aghasur**. **Brahma** knew the power of **Aghasur** and hence thought that it's impossible for any human to kill **Aghasur**, he's too powerful for even demigods. So, he wondered that how can a small shepherd kid like **Krishna** destroy powerful **Aghasur**. **Brahma** thought that this cowherd boy Krishna has deceived the innocent people of **Vrindavan** and making them fool. **Brahma** then decided to test **Krishna** and expose him in front of the people of **Vrindavan. Brahma** then came to earth. He witnessed that Krishna was eating and playing with cowherd boys. **Krishna** was also eating from their hands and was feeding them with his. **Brahma** stole all the calves when they went far while grazing. When **Krishna** and friends realized that calves have gone too far and Krishna assured them that he'll bring them back soon and went away, **Brahma** stole the cowherd boys as well by making them unconscious and he took both calves and cowherd boys with him to his Brahma Lok (The abode of **Brahma**). **Krishna**, when couldn't find calves and returned, witnessed that his friends were missing too? He could understand that this was a trick performed by **Brahma. Krishna** then started his most beautiful magical Leela, he in order to please Lord **Brahma**, as well as his own associates and their mothers, recreated all the cowherd boys along with calves who emerged from him. When one full year had passed on **Vrindavan, Brahma** returned and saw that **Krishna** was still engaged as usual with his friends and the calves and cows.

Now let's understand that **Brahma's** one day is equal to 4.32 billion years of humans so we can understand that despite of the fact that Brahma went to his lok or his place and kept the stolen boys and calves and came back with a speed much more than the speed of light within a fraction of his second, a year was passed here on earth. Meanwhile, here on earth, mothers of all boys as well as mother cows of calves were happy playing with their boys and calves with utmost affection and love. Meanwhile, here on earth, mothers of all boys as well as mother cows of calves were happy playing with their boys and calves with utmost affection and love.

This affection was not only because they were with their children but also due to the fact that those children were actually forms of **Krishna** emanated from his body and since those mothers of boys and mother cows always loved **Krishna** and wanted to adore him as their child or actually adored him as their child, they were elated and their happiness knew no bounds.

On the other hand, when **Brahma** came back to earth, what he beheld was enough to bewilder him completely. He observed that Krishna, like any other day, was having his lunch in the forest with his friends **Brahma** had just now stolen. Calves also were grazing nearby. **Brahma** couldn't believe his own eyes and got extremely baffled. He used his divine vision and observed that stolen boys and calves were still in his lok-sleeping. He again looked at **Krishna** and friends and calves. **Brahma** meditated on God and prayed to him to give him vision and knowledge to know the truth. Lord or God almighty was none other than **Krishna** and hence he showed him the truth. **Brahma** saw that all the cowherd boys and calves were Lord **Vishnu** with four hands and extreme lustrous and glittering persona. Brahma plunged in the lotus feet of Lord **Krishna**. He had realized his blunder mistake. He apologized. Within a moment, there were thousands of **Brahmas** around Krishna. Some of them had 10 heads, some had 100, some had 1000 and so on. To **Brahma's** amazement, Krishna explained him that he is **Brahma** or creator of just one universe; there are infinite universes or there are multiverses. **Krishna** told **Brahma** that since **Brahma** was under the impression that he's the only creator, he had summoned other Brahmas so that he could see and realize the truth and reality. Within a moment all Brahmas returned back to their respective universes as Krishna asked them to do so. **Brahma** of this universe apologized, and **Krishna** forgave him. All the real boys and calves were returned by **Brahma** and those emanated from Lord got dissolved in him. **Brahma** offered his obeisance in the lotus feet of Lord and praised his glory and extolled his virtues and all powerful yet most merciful personality and returned back to his **Brahma lok**.

Thus, this authentic tale from the **Mahabharata** proves beyond doubt that parallel universes exists & that each one of them has their own **Brahma** just like ours. This tale also establishes the fact that the dimension of time in this universe is relative and this was known to the mankind ages before **Einstein** proved it with his theory of relativity.

Now we will discuss about the concepts of Chathur Yugas, Manvantaras & Life cycle of **Brahma**.

The lifespan of **Brahma** lasts for 100 of his years. His 12-hour day or **Kalpa** is followed by a 12-hour night or **Pralaya** of equal length. His 100-year life is called a Mahā-Kalpa, which is followed by a Mahā-Pralaya (full dissolution).

1 day (12 hours: Kalpa) of Brahma = 4.32 billion solar years

1 Day (24 hours: Kalpa + Pralaya) of Brahma = 8.64 billion solar years

30 Days (1 month) of Brahma = 259.2 billion solar years

12 months (1 year) of Brahma = 3.1104 trillion solar years

50 years (Parardha) of Brahma = 155.52 trillion solar years

100 years (lifespan: 2 Parardha) of Brahma = 311.04 trillion solar years

100 years (lifespan) of Manu = 306,720,000 solar years (71

Mahā-Yugas)

The lifespan of the Manus (progenitors of mankind) lasts for 100 of their years. Each Manu reigns over a period called a **Manvantara**, each lasting for 71 Mahā-Yugas. In a **Manvantara**, there are 14 Indras who reign in succession. A total of 14 Manus reigns successively in one Kalpa (day of Brahma). A **Mahā Yuga** lasts for 4.32 million years, where the current is the 28th of 71.

The history of humanity is divided up into four Yugas (dharmic ages or world ages) **Satya Yuga, Treta Yuga, Dvapara Yuga and Kali Yuga**—each with a 25% decline in dharmic practices and length, giving proportions of 4:3:2:1 (e.g., Satya: 100% start; Kali: 25% start, 0% end), indicating a de-evolution in spiritual consciousness and an evolution in material consciousness. Kali Yuga is followed by Satya Yuga of the next cycle, where a cycle is called a **Chathur Yuga** (**Mahā Yuga** or Yuga Cycle).

Yuga	Span Divine Years	Span Solar Years
Satya	4800	1728000
Treta	3600	1296000
Dwapar	2400	864000
Kali	1200	432000

So Total span of a **Chathur Yuga (Mahā Yuga)** = *12000 Deva Years or 4.32 Million* **Solar Years.**

Thus, after each **Manvantara** the corresponding 7

Saptarishis & the **Manu** Changes. Within each **Manvantara Indra** or King of Devas changes 14 times & a new **Indra** gets his turn to rule over the Devas.

Thus, in this chapter we have covered all the mentioned topics about Brahma, his relationship to Brahman & established their difference with Brahmins one of the four Vargas of the caste system. We have also discussed about Chathur Yugas, Life cycle of Brahma & Manvantaras. Thus, ends this chapter.

6.   Vishnu & His Incarnations

We begin this chapter with a very famous sloka for the Bhagvada Geetha which is given below.

"Yada   yada   hi   dharmasya   glanirbhavati   bharata Abhythanamadharmasya   tadatmanam   srijamyaham, Paritranaya   sadhunang   vinashay   cha   dushkritam Dharmasangsthapanarthay sambhabami yuge yuge".

As on the date of 8/11/2020 Janmashtami I write this chapter it gives me immense pleasure to explain the meaning of these immortal slokas as said by Shri Krishna to Arjuna and recorded in **Shrimad Bhagavatam** by the great sage *Shri Krishna Dwaipyana Vedvyasa.*

Shri Krishna says as and when the righteousness will be harmed and there will be rise of the evil on this earth, I will come for the restoration of the peace, to uphold the righteousness & protection of the saintly humans through the destruction of the evil in every age.

These slokas are a promise to common men who are believers of Dharma, conduct & delivery of divine justice from the almighty **Shri Krishna**. It's a kind of assurance of the extension of protection to all those human beings who are defending their greater spiritual Dharma against the atrocities of the rising evil. This assurance is universal and is true across all the cycles of ages & independent of time. If ones heart refuses to believe & trust the divine justice of the almighty since one has suffered tremendously on this life & has not gained any materialistic success it's high time that such an individual should shed away all the rising queries and doubts on their mortal mind and focus on these slokas. Its time that such an individual should focus on only the assurance of lord Shri Krishna and understand that individual Karmas should transform through wisdom, non-violence, saintly intentions & code of conduct for the Lord's assured protection against the evil.

Hence, we should focus only on doing Karma and leave it unto **Shri Krishna** to decide the fruits & time to render the benefits of enjoyment of it. Its our eternal Dharma to dedicate our lives for the cause of dedicated service (**Nishkam Karma**) to whatever Varna (profession) God has chosen for us. Sometimes we consciously get an option to choose our profession & sometimes our profession chooses us. In either way we should constantly focus on doing our job honestly & through the ways of Dharma for the purpose of dedicated service (mode of Bhakti for **Nishkam Karma**) & leave the rest upon the Lord to decide of the worldly comforts & rewards that we deserve while discharging our duties.

It's a common human ignorance that leads us to seek for name, fame, power & all sorts of materialistic pleasures & in that process we end up in committing sins through any one of the six **Shadripu** mainly **Kama (lust), krodha (anger), lobha (greed), Mada (pride), moha (attachment), and matsarya (jealousy).** These Ripus play on our ignorance and creates illusions (**Maya**) that drives us to commit sins. *"These Ripus are the six children of mother Mahamaya on whose hands our fate plays through various illusions if we choose to remain ignorant of Shri Mahavishnu".*

Now the primary reason for which I have chosen to write this chapter is I want to unfold a secret to my readers which will shed off all their ignorance about the worldly illusion. The secret lies in front of our eyes however we have never been able to understand it. As a seeker of truth and an explorer it's my Dharma to share the knowledge that I have gained while searching for this truth and I have highlighted that in the quote I mentioned above. I have left the decoding of the secret to my truth seeker readers & I will wait for your letters anxiously when you have been able to decode it.

I am also providing the clue to decode this secret from **Shrimad Bhagavatam**. The energy of the lord called **Avidya** is the state of conditioned souls in this universe. This energy called **Avidya** manifests itself through the material nature of ignorance and resides in all conditioned souls. However, the moment we chose to devote all our services to the Lord and submit ourselves to him this **Avidya** transforms into his divine energy of **Vidya** which starts to reside as pure knowledge in conditioned souls. Thus, through continuous accumulation of **Vidya** the conditioned souls start becoming aware of the truth for which they have been conditioned. As their ignorance slowly transforms into bliss through the scientific process of **Bhakti Yoga,** they become Yogis aware of the various integration of various psychic energies & realms of this universe. Thus, they can work more effectively through the various conditional factors of this material universe and reduce their Karmic backlogs effectively through various births. This journey starts initially through the science of **Bhakti Yoga** then slowly enters the zone of **Gyan Yoga** and finally takes us slowly through the process of **Karma Yoga** to understand and be aware of the entire process of entry into this material world & exit from it. Throughout this journey as stated in **Shrimad Bhagavatam** if a devotee has completely surrendered himself unto the lord, he becomes free of any rising doubts in his mind. Thus,

Mahamaya transforms herself into **Yoga Maya** and the **Ripus** transform into their corresponding opposites for pure devotees guiding the Yogi through the process of **Nishkam Karma** towards **Moksha** or **Liberation** from the ignorance of the conditioned protocols of this material universe. Thus, curse becomes boon and every birth becomes an opportunity to know the secrets of this universe and get each step closer to the infinity.

The Lord will however continuously test our faith and submission onto him and only through continuous and persistent surrender we can succeed to devote our services unto him and let him guide us through the Yogic processes mentioned above. If we are lost as most of us often do our spiritual process is hampered and to get back again to the right path through continuous efforts the yogi must remember that the Lord is always forgiving & ready to guide us whenever we are repentant of our ignorance, misdeed & sins we have committed. We should not drown ourselves so much into guilt & shame that there is no comeback. We should be confident & ready to purify ourselves and its only if we chose to remain under this conditioned state that we will remain forever.

Thus, wise men know that guilt & shame are the weapons of the evil to mislead & imprison the conditioned souls and keep them away from the process of repentance to attain the bliss of the god.

A doomed soul is the evil alone in this universe and tries to doom other souls to create an alternate reality that will suit his reign. A doomed soul thus believes in his own version of the universe rather than the version of the Lord's universe. In Order to create the version of his universe he dooms others and keeps them away from the truth.

This chapter is an attempt to identify the truth behind each incarnations of Lord Shri Vishnu to save the doomed and bestow his protection to his devotees and the saintly beings. Thus, for explorers like us it is important to understand the truth behind each incarnation and scientifically pursue the truth of this life & the life beyond it.

Now remember the great quote in the **Peter Parker** principle of the Spiderman "**With great power comes great responsibility**". This quote is perfect to explain what true power yields in this universe. A power is an ability to fulfill our greater responsibilities towards this universe. Powers are given by Lord to discharge our dedicated services for his assigned work. The Lord takes away those powers at his will when we no longer need them or as and when our ego arises. Hence to enjoy the benefits of those powers we should not even for a moment forget that we reside in him and he resides in us & use the god given **Shakti** only to fulfill the responsibilities of this universe for which he has assigned us that task. I have discussed in detail in the previous chapter about what true Power or Shakti is and how to awaken it.

Now we will discuss in detail about the 24 Avatars or Incarnations of **Shri Vishnu,** their purposes for manifesting into the conditioned world as per the promise of the sloka mentioned at the beginning of this chapter and what they had taught us.

According to **Bhagavat Purana** Shri Vishnu have already incarnated on earth 23 times, while the 24th avatar is yet to be born as 'Kalki Avatar'. Out of these 24 avatars, 10 avatars, called as Dashavatar, are the main incarnations of Vishnu.

They are **Matsya, Kurma, Varaha, Narasimha, Vamana, Parashuram, Rama, Krishna, Buddha** and **Kalki** avatars. Of all these Avatars, Shri Krishna alone is considered a sampoorna incarnation i.e. a direct and complete representation of the supreme divine himself.

The notable fact about these Dashavatar is that out of ten forms three forms are animal forms, one half man & half lion and the rest six are human forms. Thus, what can be the greatest proof that in his creation the god is impartial and doesn't distinguish between his creations based on animals or humans. Whatever may be the form his justice is impartial. He has himself manifested in animal forms as a proof of his impartiality. The half man & animal incarnation sheds our ignorance that Lord Vishnu is not conditioned to the creations of **Brahma** alone. His Leela is infinite & if required for upholding Dharma he can take any form as per his wish and enlighten us on the path of righteousness.

The Spiritual Significance of the incarnations are summarized below.

- *All the four sages, the first incarnation was a symbol of brahmacharya (state of continence and chastity) and on the path of salvation. Brahmacharya purify conscience (i.e., manas, buddhi, chit, pride/ego).*

- *Varaha, the second incarnation is a symbol of Spiritual upliftment of this earth. Whenever this earth sinks under the demonic influences the lord emerges for its upliftment in the spiritual sky from this vast cosmic ocean.*

- *Narad ji, the third incarnation is symbol of bhakti (unselfish love). After practicing Brahmacharya and*

89

Santosh (contentment), bhakti sprouts.

- *In Nara-Narayana forms, the fourth incarnation the lord preached the dharma of guru (Narayana) and dharma of disciple (Nara) himself. He despite being the supreme goal of meditation, performed the meditation himself. He meditated on whom? He meditated on himself. Vedas say, **'patim vihvasya aatmeshvaram'** means, he who is owner/protector of the entire universe is the only owner/protector of himself.*

- *Kapil muni, the fifth incarnation was symbol of vidya (spiritual wisdom) and vairagya (detachment). Bhakti stabilizes with spiritual wisdom and vairagya.*

- *Datta, the sixth incarnation reflect that when five attributes viz. Brahmacharya, Santosh, Gyan, Bhakti and Vairagya, comes in life, one will transcend all forms of matter & beyond all properties of matter to become Gunatit, one who is above the three gunas of rajas, tamas, and sattva; above Maya.*

- *Yagna, the seventh incarnation is a ritual performed to please the gods.*

- *11th, 12th & 13th incarnations of Kurma, Dhanvantri and Mohini were for churning the cosmic ocean of life to explore gun & avgun i.e. to distinguish between purity & evil.*

- *14th incarnation of Narsimha & 17th incarnation of Sri Hari gave the message that Lord protects his devotees against all odds.*

- *In 16th incarnation of Hayagriva, the Lord sent a*

clear message of the protection of the Vedas.

- *In the 19th incarnation of **Shri Krishna Dwaipyana Vedvyasa** ji compiler of Vedas & Puranas, Parashar Hora Astrology & the only authentic documented source of Shrimad Bhagavat Geetha to record the divine teachings & priceless wisdom of Lord Shri Krishna through ages.*

- *In 15th incarnation of Vamana, 21st incarnation of Shri Rama and 22nd incarnation of Shri Krishna, the Lord re-established Dharma by liberating the doomed souls or evil & protecting his devotees and kept his promise.*

- *In 23rd incarnation of Buddha, the enlightened one taught the world non-violence, renunciation & to rise above the realities of the four-fold life for growth & expansion to attain Nirvana beyond the cycles of birth & death.*

- *In the 18th incarnation of Parashuram the lord again kept his promise of protecting the world against evil atrocities & pseudo disguised warriors through his axe of time or Parashu. He sent a clear message that evil might have thousand arms and become Sahasrabahu or Kartavirya Arjuna however one blow of the axe of time from the Lord is sufficient to destroy such an evil & restore peace and balance in this universe.*

Interestingly the Avatars take different forms: starting with a sequence of animal forms suggestive of an evolutionary order: Matsya a Fish, Kurma a Tortoise, Varaha a Boar, through Narsimha, a half-lion Man, making a transition to the human sequence of Vamana, Parashuram, Rama, Krishna and Kalki making the ten accepted by the Vaishnava tradition.

Now we will sequentially discuss about all the 24 Avatars or Incarnations of **Shri Ksirodakasayi Vishnu** on our universe. As mentioned before in the earlier chapters there are multiple parallel universes, & each has its own **Brahma** and **Ksirodakasayi Vishnu**. Each of these universes has their own calculations of **Yugas, Manvantaras & Kalpa** depending on its **Brahma**.

The Brief information about the 24 avatars are as below.

1. First incarnation was as four sages named Sanaka (ancient), Sanatana (eternal), Sanandana (ever joyful) & Sanatkumara (ever young). We have already discussed about them in the earlier chapter.

2. Second incarnation was Varaha, a boar. As per story, in ancient times when demon Hiranyaksha took the earth and hid it in the sea, then Lord Vishnu appeared in the form of **Varaha**. Lord Varaha started searching for the earth. With the help of his snout, he found the earth and by going inside the sea and placing it on his teeth, he brought the earth out. When Hiranyaksha demon saw this, he challenged the Varaha form of Lord Vishnu to battle. A fierce battle ensued in both. Finally, Lord Varaha killed Hiranyaksha. After this, Lord Varaha pillaged the water with his hooves and set the earth on it.

3. Third incarnation was Narada. Narada is one of the seven Manas sons (psyche sons, by process of thought) of Brahma. He has attained the rank of

Devrishi by hard penance. He is considered one of the exclusive devotees of Lord Vishnu.

4. Nara and Narayana were the Fourth Avatar of Lord Vishnu. The twins were sons of Dharma, the son of Brahma and his wife Murti (Daughter of Daksha) or Ahimsa. They live at Badrikashram performing severe austerities and meditation for the welfare of the world. These two inseparable sages took avatars on earth for the welfare of mankind. Legend has it that once Lord Shiva tried to bring the fame of Nara and Narayana before the entire world. To do that, he hurled his own potent weapon **Pashupathastra** at the meditating Rishis. The power of their meditation was so intense that the weapon lost its power before them. Lord Shiva stated that this happened since the duo were Jnanis of the first order constantly in the state of Nirvikalpa Samadhi. The Bhagavat Purana tells the story of the birth of Urvashi from the sages Nara-Narayana.

5. Fifth incarnation was Kapil muni. His father's name was Maharishi Kardam and mother's name was Devhooti. Kapil muni propounded Samkhya philosophy.

6. Sixth incarnation was Dattatreya. As per story, once Goddess Lakshmi, Parvati and Saraswati became extremely proud of their ancestors. God created Leela to destroy their ego. According to him, one day Narada reached Devloka while wandering around and told the three ladies in turn that your saintliness was nothing in front of

Anusuya, the wife of sage Atri. The three goddesses told this thing to their husbands and asked them to test the rituals of Anusuya. Then Lord Shankar, Vishnu and Brahma came to the ashram of Atri Muni dressed as a monk. Maharishi Atri was not in the ashram at that time. The three asked for alms to the goddess Anusuya, but also said that you must give alms to us without getting naked. At first Anusuya was shocked to hear this, but then fearing that the sadhus should not be insulted, she remembered her husband and said that if my religion is true, then these three sadhus should become children of six months. As soon as he said this, Trinity started crying as an infant. Then Anusuya became a mother and breastfed them with her arms and started swinging in the cradle. When the three gods did not return to their places, the ladies were distraught. Then Narada came there and told the whole thing. The three goddesses came to Anusuya and apologized. Then the goddess Anusuya made Trinity in her former form. Pleased, Trinity gave him a boon that all three of us would be born as sons from your womb. Then Moon was born from the part of Brahma, Durvasa from the part of Shankar and Dattatreya from the part of Vishnu.

7. Seventh incarnation was Yajna. Yajna was born in Swayanbhuva Manvantara to protect it. As per story, Akuti was born from the womb of Shatarupa, the wife of Swayanbhuva Manu.

8. Eighth incarnation was Rishabh. As per story, Maharaja Nabhi had no children. For this reason, he

performed a yajna with his wife Meru Devi, wishing for a son. Pleased with the sacrifice, Lord Vishnu himself appeared and gave a boon to Maharaj Nabhi that I will be born here as a son. After some time, Lord Vishnu Maharaj was born as a boon in the form of a son. Seeing the son's exceedingly well-structured body, fame, oil, strength, opulence, fame, might and valor, etc., Maharaj Nabhi named him Rishabh (superior).

9. Lord Vishnu in his ninth incarnation as 'Prithu' came into existence after the body of King 'Vena'. Lord Vishnu took this incarnation as per the wishes of the sages. The earth had concealed all the vegetation's within her and as a result the whole land had become barren. To protect the humanity, Lord Vishnu took incarnation as Prithu by milking the cow (earth). This is considered that as a very supreme incarnation because the earth has remained full of vegetation's after that.

10. Tenth incarnation was Matsya (fish) to save the world from destruction. As per story, King Satyavrat was taking a bath in the river one day. Suddenly a small fish came to his Anjali. When he thought to put it back in the ocean, but that fish said - you don't put me in the ocean, otherwise big fish will eat me. Then King Satyavrat kept the fish in his kamandal. When the fish became bigger, the king kept it in his lake, and then on seeing it, the fish became bigger. The king understood that this is not an ordinary creature. The king pleaded with the fish to come in real form. Hearing the king's prayer, the lord Vishnu appeared, and said that this

is my mermaid. God told Satyavrat - listen King Satyavrat! There will be a catastrophe seven days from today. Then a huge boat will come to you with my inspiration. Take the subtle body of sapta rishis, medicines, seeds, and creatures and sit in it, when your boat starts to waver, then I will come to you as a fish. At that time, you tie that boat with my horn by Vasuki Nag. At that time, I will answer you by asking questions, so that my glory which is known by the name of Param brahma will be revealed in your heart. Then, when the time came, the fishery god Vishnu preached philosophy to King Satyavrat, who is famous by the name Matsyapuran. This Satyavrat is the current 7th Manu of this universe. The Bible mentions him as Noah and the story of Noah's arc is famous worldwide.

11. Eleventh incarnation was Kurma or turtle. As per Bhagavat Purana, Shukra Acharya the guru of the demons got Sanjeevani Mantra by pleasing lord Shiva. The Mantra can be given to only one in one Kalpa. This mantra is very powerful and can heal the dead and bring them back to life. So, whenever there were conflicts between Devas and Danavas Shukracharya will bring them back to life whereas the Devas died in their hands. When Indra went to Lord Vishnu, he asked him to churn the ocean. Then Indra agreed to churn the ocean together with the demons and gods. To churn the sea, the Mandarachal Mountain was made a churner and Nagraj Vasuki was netted. The gods and demons, forgetting their differences, uprooted Mandarachal and took him towards the sea, but they could not

take him far. Then Lord Vishnu placed Mandarachal on the beach. The gods and demons made Mandarachal into the sea and made Naga king Vasuki a rope. But due to no base below Mandarachal, he started drowning in the sea. Seeing this, Lord Vishnu took the form of a giant turtle and became the basis of Mandarachal in the sea. Mandarachal started moving fast on the huge back of Lord Kurma and thus the sea churning was completed.

12. Twelfth incarnation was Dhanvantri. He is also considered as the Master of Medicines. As per story, when the gods and the demons together churned the ocean, the first poisonous poison came out of it which was consumed by Lord Shiva. After this, Uchhashrava horse, Goddess Lakshmi, Airavat elephant, Kalpa tree, Apsaras and many other gems came out of the ocean churning. At the end, Lord Dhanvantri appeared with the nectar urn.

13. Thirteenth incarnation was Mohini. As per story, during Samudra manthan, asuras and devas started fighting for Amrit (nectar). Then Lord Vishnu incarnated as Mohini to fascinate everyone. Mohini said, I will make devas and demons drink the nectar. Both agreed. The gods sat on one side and the demons on the other side. Then Lord Vishnu, who was in the form of Mohini, started singing and distributing nectar to the gods and demons. In reality he distributed all the nectar to the devas and made them immortal while the demons were charmed by her and got fooled by continuing their lustful gaze on her. The Mohini Avatar of Vishnu

gave birth to **Rahu** (attachment, desire, illusion, conspiracy, controversy) & **Ketu** (Detachment, Moksha, Knowledge, seclusion, renunciation) from the churning of the cosmic ocean and this is the most important aspect we discuss in the next chapter.

14. Fourteenth incarnation was Narsimha (half-lion man). Lord Vishnu killed Hiranyakashipu, the king of demons, with the incarnation of Narsimha. It's believed to be the fiercest incarnation of Lord Vishnu. As per story, Hiranyakashipu, considered himself stronger than God. He had a boon from Brahma that he would not die from man, god, bird, animal, neither in day, nor at night, nor on earth, nor in the sky, nor by weapon, nor by weapon. Infact no creation of Brahma could harm him. His son's name was Prahalad. Prahalad was an ardent devotee of Lord Vishnu since childhood. When Hiranyakashipu came to know about this, he became very angry and tried to convince Prahalad, but even when Prahalad did not believe Hiranyakashipu gave him the death penalty. Every time he survived. Hiranyakashipu sister Holika, who had the boon of not burning with fire, sat in a blazing fire with Prahlada. Even then, by the grace of Lord Vishnu Prahlada survived and Holika was burnt. When Hiranyakashipu was about to kill Prahlada himself, Lord Vishnu appeared from the pillar with the incarnation of Narsimha and killed Hiranyakashipu with his nails.

15. Fifteenth incarnation was Vamana. As per Vishnu purana, Prahalad's grandson Bali took control of

heaven. All the gods went to Lord Vishnu to avoid this calamity. Then Lord Vishnu said that I will be born from the womb of Devmata Aditi and will give you the kingdom of heaven. After some time, Lord Vishnu incarnated Vamana. Once when Bali was performing a great yajna, Lord Vamana went to the sacrificial fire and asked for three feet of land from King Bali. King Bali's guru Shukracharya understood the Leela of God and asked Bali not to donate. But Bali still pledged to donate three feet of land to Lord Vamana. Lord Vamana took a huge form and measured the earth in one step and the heaven in the second step. When there was no place left for the third step, Bali asked Lord Vamana to keep the step on his head. He reached Sutha Loka– the place underneath the earth by placing a foot on Bali's head. Seeing the greatness of the sacrifice, God also made him the lord of Sutha Loka. In this way Lord Vamana helped the gods and returned them to heaven.

16. Sixteenth incarnation was Hayagriva. A legend has it that during the creation, the demons Madhu-Kaitabha stole the Vedas from Brahma, and Vishnu then took the Hayagriva form to recover them. The two bodies of Madhu and Kaitabha disintegrated into twelve pieces (two heads, two, four arms and four legs). Yet another legend has it that during the creation, Vishnu compiled the Vedas in the Hayagriva form. Some consider Hayagriva to be one of the Dashavatar of the Supreme Personality of Godhead. He along with Shri Krishna, Shri Rama and Shri Narasimha is considered to be an important avatar of the Supreme Personality of

Godhead.

17. Seventeenth incarnation was Shri Hari. As per story, a powerful Gajendra lived with his arms in the valley of the mountain called Trikuta. Once he went to bathe in the pond with his arms. There a crocodile grabbed his leg and started pulling it under water. The struggle of Gajendra and crocodile continued for a thousand years. In the end Gajendra collapses and he meditates on Lord Srihari. Hearing the praise of Gajendra, Lord Srihari appeared and killed the crocodile with his chakra. Lord Srihari saved Gajendra and made him his councilor.

18. Eighteenth incarnation was Parashuram. As per story, the city of Mahishmati was ruled by the powerful Kshatriya Kartavirya Arjuna (Sahasrabahu). He was very arrogant and tyrannical. Once Agni requested him to take food. Then Sahasrabahu came in boasting and said that you can get food from wherever you want, everywhere I rule. Then Agni started burning forests. In a forest, the sage Aapava was doing penance. Agni also burnt his ashram. Enraged by this, the sage cursed Sahasrabahu that Lord Vishnu would be born as Parashuram and destroys not only Sahasrabahu but all the Kshatriyas. Thus, Lord Vishnu was born as the fifth son of Maharishi Jamadagni in the Bhargava clan.

19. Nineteenth incarnation was Maharishi Ved Vyas. He appeared as the son of the great sage Maharishi Parashar.

20. Twentieth incarnation was Hans. Once Lord Brahma was sitting in his assembly. Then his son Sanaka reached there and started discussing about the salvation of humans with Lord Brahma. Then Lord Vishnu appeared in the form of Mahahans and he removed the doubts of Sanaka Sages.

21. Twenty-first incarnation was **Maryada Purushottam** Shri Rama. In Treta Yuga, Demon King Ravana had a lot of terror. For his slaughter, Lord Vishnu was born as a son from the womb of Mother Kausalya at King Dasharatha. In this incarnation, Lord Vishnu killed many demons and lived his entire life to leave behind a legacy of dutifulness, sacrifice, piousness & righteousness. He went to exile to keep his father's promise to his stepmother of granting her any two boons she liked. Her stepmother Kaikeyi asked for Rama's exile and right to throne for her son Bharata. While suffering exile, Ravana kidnapped away his wife Sita. In search of Sita, Lord reached Lanka, where there was a fierce battle between Lord Rama and Ravana in which Ravana was killed.

22. Twenty-second incarnation was Shri Krishna. In Dwapar Yuga, Lord Vishnu took the Shri Krishna avatar. He led the war of Mahabharata, became the charioteer of Arjuna and re-narrated to him the divine knowledge of Shrimad Bhagavat Geetha.

23. Twenty-third incarnation was Lord Buddha He established the religion Buddhism.

24. Twenty-fourth incarnation would be Kalki. According to religious texts, Lord Vishnu will

incarnate as Kalki in Kali Yuga. Lord Kalki will be born at a place called Shambhala in Moradabad district of Uttar Pradesh. Kalki, riding a horse named Devadatta, will destroy the sinners from the world and re-establish religion.

Thus, end our chapter on Lord Vishnu & his incarnations. However, the journey to eternal life and the truth will continue in the upcoming chapters where we will slowly unveil the secrets of other psychic divine forces operating in the material realm of this known, however much unknown part of our human representation of this universe. We will discover the secret of the gunas and how Yogis became Gunatit by following the principle of karmic reincarnation.

7.   Shiva The Ultimate Truth

As I begin this fascinating chapter for our dear truth seekers it is important to understand *Satyam Shivam Sundaram* which means that truth is Shiva and only truth is eternal & beautiful.

As we have started unfolding more and more secrets of the cosmic truth it is important for us to understand that without Shiva this truth exploration is incomplete. Without Shiva we will not reach our destination & without Shiva we will not be able to understand why so many people in India renounce their homes, families, relatives & comforts of life and start living the life of **Aghoris** in the Samsans of Banaras, Allahabad etc. Without Shiva the Adi yogi it is impossible to understand meditation & renunciation.

We will have to also unfold the secrets of **Neelkanth, Mahadeva, Mahakal, Rudra** & of course **Ardhanarishwar.** Without understanding **Lingam, Kumbh** & **Tantra** we will not be able to unfold the three-fold cosmic truth & the psychic forces that drives these universe & all the other universes beyond. Without **Shiva** we will not be able to know **Hanuman** & without knowing **Hanuman** how will we understand Rama? Without knowing Shiva, we will not be able to know the truth of **Sanjeevani** or **Mahamrityunjaya.** Without knowing **Shiva** visiting to **Gangotri** & **Haridwar** will not lead us to enlightenment.

Lord **Shiva** is an ardent devotee of Shri **Vishnu** & without understanding the secrets and mysteries of **Shiva** a truth seeker will not be able to completely understand Vishnu. It's through the union of **Shiva** & **Vishnu** Shakti that Lord

Hanuman came on this universe and we must understand the secrets of cosmology to understand **Hanuman**. Without Shiva its difficult to know the secrets of Poison & Nectar and without Shiva its very difficult to understand the mysteries of destruction & recreation. Without Shiva there is no **Trident** & without Shiva there is no cosmic cycle of time. Without Shiva we will not be able to understand the curse of **Krishna** to **Ashwatthama** in the Mahabharata and making him Chiranjivi.

Shiva is pure **Tamas (Inertia)** & Vishnu is pure **Sattva (Protonic charge)** when these two gunas unite through the cause of pure **Rajasic** passion of **Bhakti** or **Devotion (Electronic charge)** they form the eternal incarnation of **Hanuman Ji (nucleus)** & his creation is based on the principle of **nuclear fusion**. As per Lord Rama's boon **Hanuman Ji** is Chiranjivi and will become the next **Brahma** of this universe. This means scientifically that the next **Brahma** has been chosen to be of the one born of **nuclear fusion** while the current one is born out of **nuclear fission**.

Both **fission** and **fusion** are nuclear reactions that produce energy, but the applications are not the same. **Fission** is the splitting of a heavy, unstable nucleus into lighter nuclei, and **fusion** is the process where lighter nuclei combine releasing vast amounts of energy. This means that while the current **Brahma** is creating various worlds out of his cause of birth which is **fission** & when his cosmic time & longevity ends the next **Brahma** i.e. **Hanuman Ji** will reunite the worlds through his power of **Fusion** causing them to merge in him & release huge amount of cosmic energy into this universe in the same process which will create the new worlds.

We all know that Nuclear **Fusion** are triggered through

104

Nuclear **Fission** in nuclear reactors and thus it is evident that this universe operates through the alternate cycle of birth of **Brahmas** through **Nuclear Fission & Fusion.**

Thus, **Hanuman Ji** in this reign of Brahma will rule over all the eleven Rudra, who are different forms of destruction of the evil & is mentioned as a **Rudra Avatar** himself as when this universe becomes completely self-destructive out of its energy destabilization caused by the spread of evil he will merge & destroy its various worlds by nuclear **fusion** in the corresponding cycle of **Pralaya** & then release the cosmic energy for recreation and restoring the balance of this universe. He & **Ashwatthama** will aid **Kalki Avatar** at the end of the Kalyuga to destroy the evil and recreate this universe for its preservation.

Thus, the **Brahmashir Astra** of the current **Brahma** is based on the principle of **Nuclear Fission** which **Ashwatthama** used while trying to take revenge on the **Pandavas** after the Mahabharata war for the death of his father Drona.

Now as science have mentioned to trigger **Fusion, Nuclear Fission** is essential and here comes the role of **Ashwatthama** as he is the reincarnation of one of the eleven Rudra & was born of the four parts of Yama(death), Rudra(destruction), Kama(love) and Krodha (anger). He had one Gem on his forehead which had the power of emitting extremely high frequency radioactive energy which can start a chain reaction and he engineered the same on a radioactive blade of grass to initiate a radioactive **nuclear Fission** weapon that can cause massive destruction. **Ashwatthama's** knowledge of the **Brahmashir Astra** has not helped him much in the Dwapar Yuga during the

Mahabharata however it's going to help this universe and **Kalki** Avatar to end the **Kalyuga**.

Now to Understand the trinity of the Hindu cosmic science we have started this book with **Brahma** who is not worshipped, whose cause of creation is Rajasic which at the lower levels of consciousness appears as passion & which causes desires and creates agitation in living souls to achieve that desire. He is completely the materialistic energy of the **Brahman** & pervades this universe through his energy of **Avidya** in the human & other cosmic entities.

To aid **Brahma** in the preservation of universe the eternal **Brahman** or **Garbhodakshayi Vishnu** manifested himself as **Ksirodakasayi Vishnu** in this universe and pervades as **Vidya** in all the enlightened living entities of awakened consciousness. It is through this **Vidya** as we have discussed before we come to know of the **Brahman** & our consciousness becomes free of **Maya** of all worldly illusions.

Now Shiva is the Adi Deva, which means he is the oldest and the source of all the Devas, he is **Devadidev** which means that he is the god of the gods. All the divine celestial entities worship him and look upto him for his guidance.

The eternal **Brahman** or Mahavishnu knew that once Brahma's creation starts the cosmic cycle of time its important that he manifests as **Mahakal** or the great cosmic cycle of time on this universe. Therefore, the Brahman appeared in the form of Shiva on this universe. Hence, Shiva is known as **Mahakal.** He has no origin & no end since he is the Brahman himself and he has existed on this universe even before the existence of time. Hence, Shiva is associated with **Shunya** or zero and is the state of statelessness. **Shiva** is the **Adi Yogi** which means he is the one upon whom all

106

the yogis can meditate and achieve the state of statelessness or being on the time independent platform in this universe. The Vidya of Shiva pervades time and brings Moksha or salvation to the Yogi hence Shiva is often called as **Mahadeva** the one who is the greatest of the Devas. **Shiva** is the supreme state of consciousness and hence he is the ardent devotee of Shri **Garbhodakshayi Vishnu** who is the supreme consciousness or the **Brahman** himself. Om is the audible vibration of the supreme consciousness hence Om is chanted as part of our sacred mantras. The state of supreme consciousness or **Shiva** resides in the crown chakra of human beings. Hence, during **Kundalini Yoga** when our primordial cosmic energy which resides in our root chakra moves upwards and meets the crown chakra, we become aware of the cosmic truth of this universe. To describe this mystic process of yoga or union of the soul with the universe the Yogis call it beautifully and poetically as the **Shakti** meeting the **Shiva**.

It is said that **Shiva** Loka, the abode of Lord **Shiva** exists on the Mount **Kailash** in the Himalayas. As discussed before Mount Kailash is the Crown Chakra or the Sahasrara of this earth. Thus, it is the abode of supreme consciousness or **Shiva** the ultimate truth on this earth. Thus, a Yogi who meditates after taking a bath in divine **Man Sarovar Taal (Lake)** will be able to activate his crown Chakra by the grace of the divine Lord.

He will be able to realize the ultimate truth or **Shiva** and get liberated from this endless bondage of births and deaths. He will be able to repay all his Karmic debts by the grace of the divine god through his bhakti and become a free unconditioned soul.

Shiva is truth and the only cycle of truth is the cycle of destruction and recreation. Thus, **Shiva** or **Rudra** works over the dissolution of the material nature at the end of **Manvantaras** or the divine cycle of time.

Now we will come to the fact that how Shiva chose to be **Rudra**. Let us recall from the Bhagavat Purana which mentions that **Brahma** is the director in charge of the mode of passion of material nature. Therefore, it was natural for him to become angry on the refusal of his sons the Sanad Kumaras to obey his order. Although the Kumaras were right in such acts of refusal, **Brahma**, being absorbed in the mode of passion, could not check his passionate anger. He did not express it, however, because he knew that his sons were far enlightened in spiritual advancement, he should not express his anger before them. Although he tried to curb his anger, it came out from between his eyebrows, and a child mixed blue and red was immediately generated.

Now the face of anger is the same whether exhibited due to ignorance or knowledge. Although Brahma tried to curb his anger, he could not do so, even though he is the supreme being. Such anger in its true color came from between the eyebrows of Brahma as **Rudra**, in a mixed color of blue (ignorance) and red (passion), because anger is the product of passion and ignorance.

Now **Shiva** as we have discussed before is the state of supreme consciousness of the eternal Brahman and hence is the **Brahman** himself. The creator of **Brahma** i.e. the **Brahman** knew that all the creations of **Brahma** will not be untouched from his ignorance or **Avidya** which resides in his mode of passion and will ultimately invoke the egocentric fragile spiritual degradation in all of his creations.

The **Brahman** thus bonded to his creation i.e. **Brahma** manifested himself in the **Tamas** of this universe as inertia and became the **Mahakal** or the cosmic truth of time himself. Having discussed about the **Mahakal** earlier in this chapter it should be now clear to readers that the creation of **Rudra** from between the eyebrows of **Brahma** as the result of his anger, generated from the mode of passion partly touched by ignorance, is very significant. It was the demand of the time or the **Mahakal** and hence **Shiva** manifested himself as **Rudra** and expressed his worldly form through the principle of **Rudra** in this universe.

Brahma gave to him the residences: the heart, the five senses, the organs of the action & the mind. Thus, in total **Brahma** designated eleven places to Rudra.

Hence having designated eleven places in total **Rudra** took the form **Ardhanarishwar** which means he incarnated as half primordial cosmic **Purusha** & half primordial cosmic **Prakriti**. The **Purusha** then split himself into eleven male forms of Rudra named Manyu, Manu, Mahinasa, Mahan, Siva, Ṛtadhvaja, Ugrareta, Bhava, Kala, Vamadeva & Dhṛtavrata. Similarly, the **Prakriti** split herself into eleven female forms of Rudrani or consorts of Rudra named Dhi, Vrtti, Usana, Urna, Niyuta, Sarpis, Ila, Ambika, Iravatl, Sudha, Diksha. Thus, the **Prakriti** is the primordial cosmic goddess and is known as **Adi Shakti**.

The Shiva Purana describes that the creator **Brahma** created all male beings, the Prajapati, and told them to regenerate, which they were unable to do. Confronted with the resulting decline in the pace of creation, Brahma was perplexed and contemplated on Shiva for help. To enlighten **Brahma** of his folly, Shiva appeared before him as **Ardhanarishwar**.

Brahma prayed to the female half of Shiva to give him a female to continue creation. The goddess agreed and created various female powers from her body, thereby allowing creation to progress.

In **Bhagavad-Geetha** the principle of Rudra is described beautifully. Krodha (anger) is the product of Kama (lust), which is the result of the mode of passion. When lust and hankering are unsatisfied, the element of krodha appears, which is the formidable enemy of the conditioned soul. This most sinful and inimical passion is represented as the false egocentric attitude of thinking oneself to be all in all. Such an egocentric attitude on the part of the conditioned soul, who is completely under the control of material nature, is described in **Bhagavad-Geetha** as foolish.

The egocentric attitude is a manifestation of the **Rudra** principle in the heart, wherein krodha (anger) is generated. This anger develops in the heart and is further manifested through various senses, like the eyes, hand, legs.

When a man is angry, he expresses such anger with red-hot eyes and sometimes makes a display of clenching his fists or kicking his legs. This exhibition of the Rudra principle is the proof of Rudra's presence in such places. When a man is angry, he breathes very rapidly, and thus Rudra is represented in the air of life, or in the activities of breathing. When the sky is overcast with dense clouds and roars in anger, and when the wind blows very fiercely, the Rudra principle is manifested, and so also when the sea water is infuriated by the wind it appears in a gloomy feature of Rudra, which is very fearful to the common man.

When fire is ablaze, we can also experience the presence of Rudra, and when there is an inundation over the earth, we can understand that this is also the representation of Rudra. There are many earthly creatures who constantly represent the **Rudra** element. The snake, tiger and lion are always representations of Rudra. Sometimes, because of the extreme heat of the sun, there are cases of heatstroke, and due to the extreme coldness created by the moon there are cases of collapse.

There are many sages empowered with the influence of austerity and many yogis, philosophers and renouncers who sometimes exhibit their acquired power under the influence of the **Rudra** principle of anger and passion. When the Rudra principle is exhibited by persons who are not engaged in the devotional service of the Supreme Personality of Godhead, the angry person falls from the peak of his improved position.

Thus, when the creations of **Brahma** out of their continuous ignorance of **Avidya** engage themselves in the material mode of passion i.e. **Rajas** and gets bonded through the **Tamas** of committing continuous sins, the Purity of **Vidya** gets diminished in the universe which causes the **Sattvic** Guna of the universe to become lesser. Hence the **Vidya** or the Lord of the **Sattva** Guna i.e. Vishnu himself incarnates in those times to preserve the balance of the universe and prevent the spread of the evil of ignorance further which can harm the spiritual progress of reaching the state of supreme consciousness i.e. **Shiva.**

This is the reason that Shiva took the form of **Rudra** and emerged through the wrath of **Brahma** so that he can work in coordination with Vishnu and destroy the Evil of Ignorance & give the sinners another chance for Moksha by the process of rebirth. Those who are only pure devotees will be preserved by the incarnations of Lord Vishnu & the sinners will be destroyed by the incarnations of Rudra/Shiva.

Shiva's trident or **Trishool** is a symbol of balance & has three **shools** each of which stands for:

1. *The Heavenly abodes or Swarga Loka*

2. *The Earthly abodes or Martyaloka*

3. *The Lower Worlds or Patala Loka*

Shiva's trident also stands for Sattva, Rajas & Tamas Gunas. Thus, Shiva has complete control over the three Gunas and during the complete annihilation of **Pralaya** he can dissolve all the worlds created by **Brahma**. Only the **Vaikuntha** or the **Vishnu Loka** which is the abode of Lord Vishnu on this universe cannot be destroyed by Shiva. Thus, only the devotees of **Lord Shri Vishnu** will be pardoned by Shiva as he himself is his devotee and he work in coordination with him so the rest of the worlds will be annihilated by him.

As and when Lord Vishnu incarnates on this earth it is evident that Shiva may also incarnate for his aid in preserving his devotees and destroying the evil of egocentric Brahma's creations to send them towards the direction of **reincarnation** or **regeneration**. Thus, during **Samudra Manthan** when Lord Vishnu took Kurma Avatar Shiva took the incarnation of **Neelkanth** & swallowed all the poisons.

All the chaos in this universe are initiated by the boon of **Brahma** and sometimes by the intentional boons given by **Shiva** to the ignorant & greedy devotees of **Rudra** which ultimately leads to their downfall and destruction in the hands of **Vishnu**.

Thus, it is easy to please **Bholenath** at the material level as it will seem like he will be satisfied with a superficial **Bhakti** and simple religious techniques, however at the cosmic spiritual layer, remember he is still the **Mahakal** and he has the past, the present and the future of the devotees at his control. He is himself the cause & the effect.

So, he knows everything transcendental about the devotee and the cause for which the native is worshipping him & accordingly he knows the effect. Hence he might not judge the devotee immediately but rather choose to judge him in the long run by giving him a shakti in the form of a boon to see what kind of a practice the devotee might engage after getting the boon. If the devotee engages in evil practices and violates the **Peter Parker** principle described in the earlier chapter, the **Rudra** will then destroy him to regenerate & give another chance through a boon to invoke his inner **Shiva** or the state of supreme consciousness.

The same thing happened with **Ravana** the urdent devotee of **Lord Shiva** who out of his ignorance & ego of **Brahma's** boon refused to follow any religious principles of the universe. He kidnapped somebody else's wife for his revengeful attitude thinking that ordinary human being who follows religious practices & boundaries of **Maryada** are powerless in front of him. His sins lead him to the final destruction in the hands of **Maryada Purushottam Shri Rama** aided by the **Rudra Avatar Shri Hanuman.** Readers can try to Recollect the curse of Jaya & Vijaya the gatekeepers of Vaikuntha by the Kumaras for they were born as **Ravana** and **Kumbhakarna**. This will help to connect the dots. Lord Vishnu kept his promise to his gatekeepers & freed them from their cursed birth by incarnating as Shri **Rama** and Lord Shiva incarnated as

Hanuman to aid him in this adventure since **Ravana** became more arrogant under the **Maya** of his power after satisfying Lord Shiva.

Thus, Shiva alone is the truth of the cycle of destruction & recreation & presides over the eleven Rudra to regulate the life cycle of the Jivatmas through this eternal truth. Now that we understood *Satyam Shivam Sundaram* let us move on to the legacy of **Sanjeevani** & **Mahamrityunjaya.**

Hindu sacred scriptures have many incredibly powerful Mantras. When Mantras are chanted with utmost devotion, they yield beneficial results. Nonetheless, some Mantras are secretly shared by the Gods to their devotees. One such Mantra is the **Sanjeevani**, that was given to **Shukracharya** by none other than Lord Shiva. **Sanjeevani** Mantra is a potent Mantra that can infuse life into the dead. In short, it is a Mantra that gives life or a new lease of life to the deceased.

There was a son of **Brahma** named Angiras who was one of the Saptarishis and his students were the most renown. He had a son **Brihaspati,** and his most brilliant student was Shukra. The Devatas are entities inclined to Sattvic and Rajasic energies. So, these Devatas went to Angiras and asked him to refer his best student to be their Dev Guru. Angiras knew that the best was Shukra, but fatherly interest intervened, and he instead sent **Brihaspati** to be the Dev Guru. This hurt Shukra deeply and on a rebound, went and offered his services to the Demons (enemies of the Devatas) and became known as Daityaguru **Shukracharya.**

Shukracharya hung upside down from a tree and gave up food and water. He survived on the smoke coming from

114

burnt leaves on the ground. Lord Shiva wanted to test both Indra (the King of Gods) and **Shukracharya** by giving them the task. Indra decided not to take part in it while **Shukracharya** volunteered to do it. He knew that he would be able to live up to Lord Shiva's expectations, while Indra believed that the sage would lose his life midway. However, after realizing that **Shukracharya** may pass the test, a complacent Indra made several attempts to disrupt the task. In the end, his daughter Jayanti volunteered to ruin the sage's efforts. Therefore, she added chilies to the burnt leaves to make sure **Shukracharya** feels suffocated. But her attempt turned futile as the sage continued to perform the task. Blood oozed from his eyes, nose, and mouth, but he remained determined to complete the test. Nonetheless, when Lord Shiva saw **Shukracharya's** endurance and will power, he intervened and stopped the test. And out of admiration for his efforts, Lord Shiva decided to bless **Shukracharya's** with the **Sanjeevani** Mantra. Lord Shiva was pleased with **Shukracharya's** devotion and will power. Moreover, he knew that the sage truly deserved it because he showed humility as a genuine devotee and was courageous enough to face all the odds. However, before giving it to **Shukracharya**, Lord Shiva warned him not to misuse it. Thus, by saying so, he asked **Shukracharya** to make constructive use of the Mantra, i.e., for the welfare of the humans however, **Shukracharya** who wanted to avenge the Devas for humiliating him used it for the welfare of the Danavas. This eventually led to the **Kurma** & **Mohini** Avatars of Lord Vishnu during Samudra Manthan and covered in the last chapter.

Mahamrityunjaya mantra is addressed to Shiva for warding off untimely death. It is also chanted while smearing ashes over various parts of the Body and utilized in reciting or performing Yagna to get desired results. While its energy protects and guides, initiates a mantra re-links consciousness to its deeper & more abiding nature. Repetition of the mantra constitutes recitation, the practice of which develops concentration that leads to complete transformation of awareness.

It is said to be beneficial for mental, emotional, and physical health and to be a moksha mantra which bestows longevity and immortality. According to some puranas, the **Mahamrityunjaya** Mantra has been used by many rishis as well as Sati during the time when Chandra suffered from the curse of Prajapati Daksha. By reciting this mantra, the effect of the curse of Daksha, which could make him die, slowed, and Shiva then took Chandra and placed it upon his head. Hence Shiva is also called as **Chandrasekhar** the one who holds Chandra or Moon on his head.

Mrikandu, one of the strong devotees of Lord Shiva was very upset as he was childless. He knew that Lord Shiva can change his destiny and he decided to pray devotedly to Lord Shiva to make him happy and get his blessings. **Mrikandu** and his wife took a long penance in hope of getting boon of child from Lord Shiva. Impressed with their devotion, Lord Shiva blessed them with a child but also warned him that the child will be short lived. With the blessing of Lord Shiva, **Mrikandu** had a son soon who was named **Markanday** but on his birth, the priest told the couple that **Markanday** had only 12 years to live. Rishi's happiness turned into sadness, but he also assured his wife that Lord Shiva who has given birth to their child will take care of him also as he has the power to change destinies. When **Markanday** started growing up, the father gave him the initiation of Shiva Mantra. **Markanday's** mom who was always worried told

116

Markandey about his short life when he insisted to know the reason of their sadness. **Markanday** who wanted to keep his parents happy decided that he will take blessings of long life from Lord Shiva and for the same he decided to penance himself in front of **Shiva Lingam**. He created and chanted the **Mahamrityunjaya** Mantra continuously. On, his 12th birthday, when Lord Yama's messenger came to Earth to take Markanday with them, they found him too absorbed in the prayer. They waited for him for a while but then returned without him. Then Lord Yama came himself to Earth to take Markanday with him but seeing him, Markandey wrapped himself to **Shiva Lingam** and surrendered himself to the mercy of Lord Shiva. When Yama tried to snatch Markanday away from **Shiva Lingam**, Lord Shiva emerged angrily & ordered Yama to retreat as **Markanday** is his devotee & is under his protection. Lord Shiva then blessed **Markanday** with a long life. Yama promised that going forward he will never disturb anyone chanting the **Mahamrityunjaya** Mantra.

In times of distress and failure, the **Mahamrityunjaya** mantra is said to uplift people from the trap of failure and rejuvenate them to think about the purpose of their life. It is said to be a healing force that works throughout the world. **"Maha"** which means Great, **"Mrityun"** means Death and **"Jaya"** mean Victory which turns into Conquer or victory over death. It is also known as "Rudra Mantra" or "Trayambakam Mantra". Reciting the Mantra regularly and keeping the same in home, creates a positive aura all around and blesses one with long life.

Shiva is associated with Agni Tattva, the element with the power of transformation. When fire touches any solid matter, it burns it and transforms it into ash. Hence ash or **Bibhuti**, is considered spiritually as the purest form of a solid matter as it has been purified by the Agni and transformed. Thus, Yogis consider Bibhuti or ashes as an important part of their **Sadhana**. People renounce their family & homes and become ascetics to find Shiva & they apply **Bibhuti** on their bodies to purify themselves so that they can become Yogis and their quest for truth finds its way to Shiva. This is the mystery behind ashes and Shiva.

At the end of this chapter, I leave it on my readers to identify few other mysteries of Shiva like the **Aghoris** & the way of **Tantra Shakti**. However, the most important point about **Rudra** is that he is the tempest or like the strongest of the storm. For all the warriors who take up arms for defending Dharma must worship Rudra for giving them the required strength to ensure the victory of Dharma over the evil.

Dear readers & all my patriotic brothers & sisters read the below Bhajan and absorb it in your mind and heart when you are on the verge of taking a decision of what is right & what is wrong for the country for yourself and for this universe.

"Deha Shiva Var mohe hain subhkarman te kabhie na daroon, na daroon arso jab jaye ladoon nischai kar apni jeet karoon".

8. The Absolute Universal Vibration Paramatma

Brahma Vidya is the science of knowing the eternal **Brahman** and acquiring this knowledge gives a Yogi a complete understanding of the cosmic vibration existing in all the living beings of this universe. This vibration or **Om** is the vibration of the Paramatma. We as **Brahmins** are the students of this Vidya. Thus, a true Brahmin is one who is only interested about knowing the science of **Brahma Vidya** & dedicates his entire life for the purpose of studying it scientifically and follow the required practices and rituals to absorb it spiritually. Once the **Brahmin** acquires this Vidya its his responsibility to pass this transition to his disciples as a Guru and contributes to the spiritual growth of the society. I have chosen to write this book as a Brahmin for the same reason as mentioned in my initial note as an author.

Just like a photon has a dual nature the **Om** too has a dual nature of being a wave & a particle. The **Om** which resides inside the **Jivatmas** has this concentrated particle nature. The **Om** which resides in the Paramatma has this pure wave nature. Just like the photons travel with the speed of light therefore when our atman chants the **Om** of the Paramatma it connects with it at a cosmic spiritual level and the **Om** or the particle nature of our atman transcends to the wave nature and reaches the Paramatma at a speed faster than that of the light. Om sound is the primordial sound and is called the **Shabda-Brahman** (Brahman as sound). The syllable **Om** is composed of the three sounds a-u-m and the symbol's threefold nature is central to its meaning. It represents several important triads:

> The trinity of the Brahma-Vishnu & Shiva.

> The three cosmic realms of The Heavens, The Earthly planets & The Lower Worlds.

> The Three states of the consciousness conscious, subconscious & the super conscious.

> The Three-dimensional nature of time past, present & future.

Om is the first sound that came out from the mouth of **Brahma** and hence is believed to be the vibration of the Paramatma himself. Just like a new-born baby utters the first sound which relates to its mother therefore it's believed that the first sound uttered by **Brahma** relates to his creator the eternal **Brahman** or the **Paramatma**. While its symbol is recognized by most, much fewer know what the combination of curves, crescent, and dot, which make up **Om's** visual representation, stand for. Each aspect of the visual form of Om signifies a state of reality. The large lower curve marks the normal waking state. In, this condition, the mind identifies with the physical body and perceives the world through the senses. The upper curve indicates the unconscious state, or that of deep sleep. This is a state of total unawareness, in which we are in a deep dreamless sleep, and you are withdrawn from both physical and mental activities. The middle curve denotes the dream state. The dream state is in between the deep sleep and waking state, where a person explores the subconscious. Your consciousness is turned inwards, as your fears, hopes, and desires manifest themselves in an imaginary world. The dot is a symbol of enlightenment. In this state, a person becomes harmonized with the Absolute, recognizing that all of creation is made up of spirit and is united through that commonality. This state is beyond the mundane senses and can only be achieved by associating with spiritual energy.

The crescent represents **Maya**, which separates the three curves from the dot. **Maya** is the illusion that binds an individual soul to the material world. By chanting **Om**, one can transcend the three curves of material consciousness, and attain the dot of enlightenment.

The **Sankha** is a conch shell from the Indian Ocean which has spiritual significance for Hindus and Buddhists alike. It exists in two varieties. The first spirals to the right and is associated with Vishnu. The second spirals to the left and is associated with Shiva. **Om** is its sound, and as such echoes some of the most elemental aspects of life, within the spiritual universe as expressed in Hindu tradition and texts. The Om represents the atman and its union with the Brahman or the Paramatma. It is for the same reason that Vishnu holds a **Sankha or a conch shell** in one of his hands. As discussed previously the **Conch** symbolizes the announcement or the birth of the audible sound from the inaudible cosmic vibration and represents the purity of speech in living creatures.

As discussed previously there are two different ways of understanding the eternal & all-pervading **Brahman or Paramatma** which transcends over all universal entities (living, non-living & dead). These two ways are known as **Dvaityavad** or **Advaityavad**. **Dvaityavad** means duality and it agrees that the eternal **Brahman** has both formless and formed nature. So **Dvaityavad** considers both the material & the energy form of the same cosmic entity & is a more practical approach. **Dvaityavad** also considers both the law of conservation of energy & that different forms of energy are interconvertible while their integration remains constant. Thus, mostly the **Dvaityavad** followers are the devotees of Shri **Vishnu** and sees this universe as his Leela.

Advaityavad endorses non-dualism and focuses on only one aspect of the eternal **Brahman** & our unidirectional relationship to him only in the phase of complete dissolution of this universe. Thus, mostly the **Advaityavad** followers may be the devotees of Lord **Shiva** and believes that the whole universe is nothing but wave. It is just one wave (**Advaitya**) & the **Damru** of Lord **Shiva** signifies the non-dual nature of the universe during its final **dissolution**. The sound from **Damru** symbolizes the sound that originated the creation and perpetuates the universe known as **Nada**.

Thus, the **Paramatma** or **Shiva** manifested in this universe & expressed himself in the first cosmic sound of **Om** through the mouth of **Brahma**. **Shiva** holding the **Damru** is the mystic representation of the **Om**. Hence when we say _Om Namah Shivay_ it means that we are offering our obeisance to **Shiva** who is the Omkar or the aum himself. This is the truth alone & there is no other truth as beautiful as Shiva or the **Om**.

The **Nada Yoga** Philosophy believes all things -organic or inorganic -consists of **Nada**. Through meditation on **Om** the Yogi creates space for the cosmic sound and arouses the cosmic vibration residing inside him. Hence Paramatma resides in all Jivatmas through the cosmic vibration of **Om**. **Nada** is the Sanskrit word for "sound" or tone. There are two types of Nada **Ahata** which is the external sound perceived by the mind & **Anahata** which is the internal sound perceived by the heart chakra.

In the Yoga Sutras of Patanjali, Aum (Om) refers to as a

cosmic sound continuously flowing in the ether, unutterable by any human voice, fully known only to the illuminated. Further Patanjali says deep concentration on Aum is a means of liberation. None can escape a continuous communion with **Om** as it pervades the consciousness and every fiber and atom of every being. Super conscious chanting, however, is that in which the mind is deeply directed to the repetition of, and the actual profound listening to, the cosmic sound as it vibrates in the ether. This is the true way of contacting **Paramatma** as he is expressed in his creation. The chanting should be firstly loudly, then softly and then gently until it is inaudible. Hence **Aum** is referred to as **Anahata Nada** as it is a spiritual vibration and is felt at inner depths of realization of the mind. By continuously chanting **Aum** a Yogi can cure any cosmic imbalances or impurity of the Chakra System. The heart Chakra becomes completely purified by the **Anahata Nada** and becomes more capable of giving & receiving the divine love & happiness.

Man displays in himself the three divine cosmic manifestations. His Body is the result of Aum or Cosmic Vibrations at an organic level. His intelligence or the way it perceives this universe is situated in his omniscient spiritual eye located at the third eye chakra at the forehead and between the eyebrows & is perceived when awakened at an intuitive or Psychic level. The soul is just a reflection of this divine intelligence and resides at the center of the thousand petaled lotus at the **Sahasrara**.

Now the question comes is why the **Sahasrara** has been described as a thousand Petaled Lotus. The answer is that there are layered nerves & the brain can be poetically seen as a Lotus with many layers like the Petals. The **atman** or the consciousness is centered at that Lotus. By focusing the ever vibrating agitated & our restless mind on that consciousness which is the atman or the true self within us, we can know the **Paramatma**. Thus, our mind or manas is the true Ego & usually clouds our intellect located in our third eye chakra which in terms doesn't let the Sun of our **atman** situated in the **Sahasrara** to Shine. Once the mind or the manas is continuously focused on the **atman** or the true self and binds itself to it through the vibration of **Aum (Om)** the mind dissolves with the intelligence gradually and we become aware of the truth which is **Shiva** or the **Paramatma** himself. Once the mind completely dissolves with the intellect the **Mental Body** or the ego dissolves with the **Cosmic Body** and becomes one with the **Nirvanic Body of the Sahasrara**.

The **Egocentric Mind or Manas** is the root cause of all worldly illusions as the effect of **Maya** creates agitation in it and invokes the **Rajasic Ego** or perception of self and the native forgets his own true cosmic nature of the atman. Thus, the native completely ignorant of its true nature and unable to perceive the vibration of **Aum** inside him gets lost in an endless cycle of birth and death. The mother **Maya** grips his manas and he is completely lost in her Love and unable to understand the consequences of his Ego leading him to the float around in the vast oceans of this cosmos.

His quest for **Om** only begins when he has lost something worldly however at a superficial level mother **Maya** again nourishes him by replacing his need for **Om** with something else worldly which satisfies his senses and he choses to remain away from the truth or **Shiva** once again. The native is trapped in an endless cycle of births and rebirths only to be nourished by his mother **Maya** which just focuses on providing nourishment to his worldly needs and motivates him to keep focusing on them and continue all his struggle in achieving them. Thus, materialistically he strives to create a better universe around him but spiritually fails to realize that he is just part of the game or Leela and playing in the hands of Lord's materialistic energy mother **Maya.**

Maya is benevolent, she is there at every step hearing and listening to our worldly needs and has a plan for all of us to provide them and then take them away. Just like a mother plays with her children mother **Maya** plays with us too by continuously providing one toy after another and then replacing each toy with another one by the desires of **Rajas** to keep her children bounded by **Tamas** or inertia towards the **Rajasic Guna** of this universe. Thus, we are all **Tamasic Rajasic** which makes us worldly creatures. If only one can bind the **Tamas** or inertia of **Om** to the **Sattvic** Guna or pure intellect of this universe one can enter the realm of **Shiva** & **Vishnu** which is **Tamasic Sattvic**. Thus, to be aware of the truth that the mother's care and nourishment can only fulfill the emotional needs of the **Yogi** & she is just a magnetic inertia towards the vast emotional universe the **Yogi** will have to search for his father or his creator who is responsible for providing the spiritual nourishment and lead him to his true self and the purpose of his life for which he created him. As the Yogi prepares to search for his father the Paramatma or Shri **Vishnu** and become aware of the eternal truth known as **Shiva** mother **Maya** who is the consort of his father blesses him and gives him the Vidya of time or **Kala** which renders realization to his mind or manas that the time has come for his reunion with his truth. The Father then takes over the role for providing the spiritual nourishment to the Yogi and he travels from the magnetic world of emotions and illusions to another magnetic world of truth &

125

spirituality. During this process of transition mother **Mahamaya** becomes **Yoga Maya** and aids the **Yogi** to make the journey smooth for him by providing him with the needed resources for the journey. Thus, the **Yogi** automatically transcends **Maya** and rises above all worldly illusions. He becomes **Gunatit** and unites with the Infinity. Once the **Atman** dissolves in the **Paramatma, Moksha** is attained. Dear readers we as Yogis need to be aware of the **Paramatma** by continuously focusing our mind on our intellect or the true self through the process of Yoga or integration with oneself. It is for the same reason that **Shri Krishna** asks **Arjuna** to only focus on him and forget everything else. **Arjuna** by focusing on Shri Krishna will only focus on the **Paramatma** or the eternal **Brahman** which in terms will automatically destroy all his ignorance and will make him rise above **Maya** and become aware of the true form of **Lord Shri Krishna** who is the creator, protector and destroyer of all the universes and creates Brahmas & takes over the role of **Vishnu** & **Shiva** whenever he desires. Mother **Maya** or his Shakti can take over the roles of **Lakshmi** or **Parvati** to provide *Prosperity & Fulfillment when he is acting as a Protector* and *Power Desire & Ego when he is acting as a Destroyer.*

If we look at the process biologically then scientifically speaking this world becomes holistically organized into Organic & Inorganic levels only. The universe is constantly striving to create an equilibrium under this model at all levels whether it is Organic or Inorganic. All the changes are caused at the atomic levels of Organic or Inorganic objects for the cause of achieving equilibrium. Bonds are made and broken at a cellular & atomic level as an effect of the cause of achieving equilibrium under the randomness or chaos of this universe. At a subtle energy level, the randomness predominates, and this randomness or restlessness of the universe is the actual form of **Maya** hidden from us due to the illusion of her projecting temporary **Stability** created by the process of **Bonding** to achieve **Equilibrium** at a subtle energy level of the depths of Organic and Inorganic natures of consciousness. These are facts which are explained at a chemical level and studied in Chemistry however unless we chose to travel the path of Yoga, we won't be able to make any sense of it at an intellectual level of spirituality.

As Organic bonds or molecules organize itself into cells, tissues, & organs the biochemical reactions become more complex giving rise to complex DNAs & RNAs at an Organismic level. New Species are born and through the process of evolution achieves the maximum Equilibrium & eventually becomes extinct due to the randomness of the universe which causes changes at its various levels.

New species are born again, and the same cycle continues. This randomness predominates over the cycle of time or **Kala** as uncertainty and hence the **Mahakal** or **Shiva** is often seen to be in meditation to keep his randomness/**Shakti(female consort of Shiva in the form of Parvati)** at a minimum differential or delta which keeps this uncertainty at its lowest. Whenever the **Mahakal** or the Adi Yogi discontinues his meditation uncertainty increases over this universe as at those times the dance of **Shakti with Shiva** predominates which is felt as a randomness at this universe and pervades over the dimension of time or **Kala** as uncertainty. Remember **Heisenberg's** uncertainty principle *"The uncertainty principle says that we cannot measure the position (x) and the momentum (p) of a particle with absolute precision. The more accurately we know one of these values, the less accurately we know the other"*. This rule is self-explanatory as when the uncertainty increases the **Tamas** or the Inertia binds itself more and more towards the predominating **Rajas** or Desire. In such times hence the position of the Organism or the height of his Consciousness cannot be simultaneously measured along with the speed & direction of his desire multiplied with his Ego centric material existence.

At an Inorganic level elements, compounds and mixtures are formed due to this randomness and the need to create bonds for attaining stability or equilibrium. Thus, at an Inorganic atomic level this consciousness becomes more prominent. Science talks about these phenomena in the books of chemistry and explains the chemical reactions. However, at the bottom of these chemical reactions the science of consciousness and the need to form bonds for equilibrium prevails. When the inorganic combines with the Carbon, Hydrogen & Nitrogen they transform towards Organic nature and form complex Proteins. Proteins or Amino Acids & the carbohydrates are the basis of Organic creation. Through the laws of science, we combine the Inorganic building blocks into complex technologies or techniques that provides utilization & automation to mankind. Physical technologies are combined to provide robust business Infrastructures and invent complex software to manage them at a subtle layer. The internet and the networking technologies has united the whole world into a common virtual platform.

As more and more complex software emerges to support robust business transactions & virtualization, man has managed to rapidly multiply time and convert it into resources through this virtual world. If we carefully observe, then we are not inventing something new or some new technologies. These technologies or techniques are already existing in nature & we are simply observing them and learning from nature and implementing them in our daily lives to suit our needs. A scientist or an inventor is thus an awakened **Atma** who can connect with the Universe and relate themselves to it. An invention is simply an exploration from unknown towards the known. As universe slowly unfolds its secrets to the one trying to understand it through their explorations known as experiments great innovations or inventions come out. It is like the process of churning the cosmic ocean and get the best out of it. Thus, science and its experiments are a part of the **Brahma Vidya** only however at a material level only. When the results of the experiments are not as pleasant & incompatible, we can feel that the poison due to churning has come out of the etheric ocean & when time swallows that poison of unpleasantness or incompatible results a new venture starts therein to uncover another truth behind it. Thus, introspection, retrospection & Inferences are part of scientific experiments and when successful can restore happiness however only at a materialistic level of consciousness.

When the introspection goes beyond the materialistic levels of consciousness the scientist starts going into the depths of the real **Brahma Vidya.** That's where great scientists like **Oppenheimer & Einstein** can relate to the truth beyond the senses and get an opportunity to connect to the **Paramatma** or the infinity. The **Paramatma** or the **Brahman** wants us to realize the happiness of creativity and hence he created this universe for us & the **Brahma** to help us feel the joy of connecting to him through the power of our creation. As we increasingly become aware of this truth, we are getting each step closer to him in the form of **Shiva.** Then finally you recognize that you are not the Tattvas or Gunas either, &

experience yourself as:

- **SAT – Truth**

- **CHIT – Consciousness**

- **ANANDA – Bliss**

As the **Jivatmas** become increasingly aware of this truth each moment they are feeling this joy, happiness & bliss of connecting to the **Paramatma**. Their consciousness is continuously transformed, and they are lost in this eternal joy of being one & with the **Paramatma**. Thus, **Yogis** consider this world as a dream or the subconscious state of the **Paramatma or Mahavishnu** formed by his desires for us to realize the joy of creation and at the end become one and united with him. Our lives are just like living the characters inside a dream where all the story & the roles are created by the dream maker or the **Paramatma**. As **Mahavishnu** wakes up from his **Yoganidra** the dream dissolves and so do we. This is a classical way of the **Yogis** to become united with the **Paramatma** by managing their thinking to pay least attention to the superficial details of the circumstances around them and thus focus their attention & meditate more towards **Om**. There are different ways of approaching the same problem & every **Yogi** invents some other way around to get along with the truth. However whatever approach the **Yogi** may choose to reach to the truth and teach the same to his followers or disciples we must understand that truth is one & universal however due to various approaches might appear in different forms to different people. The duty of the explorers of truth is to avoid any misunderstanding with a description of one religion to attain God which might not match with another description or version of another religion for the same. We must remember that based on geographical regions and languages spoken across various parts of the world different communities have emerged through different ages and all of their versions perceived by their respective **Yogis** are true and leads to the direction of the same truth. Its therefore not wise for the followers to engage in just the interpretation of linguistic or cultural mode of different transitions by various **Gurus** & judge superficially the truth based on comparison of one version with another. The followers to become the true **Yogis** themselves must walk on the same path as shown by their **Gurus** to realize the truth and become one & united with the **Paramatma**. Crossing the cultural & linguistic barriers are an important step in the life of a **Yogi** as the first and foremost understanding of the **Yoga** comes when a human being realizes that all other humans are the children of same mother **nature** who has just different ways of expressing herself in different seasons and different places of this world.

Now as & when Yogis collectively look at a truth and agree to it, the collective vibration & its frequency starts vibrating with the frequency of the universe. Thus, with this kind of approach it's not just an individual that connects with the **Paramatma** but an entire community that connects to him and in this process all of them collectively gets benefitted by attaining the happiness & bliss and sharing the same among themselves which multiplies it further. This is the approach that most of the **Gurus** follow to teach the truth and lead their people and community towards spiritual enlightenment by connecting with the **Paramatma** through the Yogic way of **Sat Sang**.

This is an approach to speed up the process of **Moksha** by leading more people towards it. This approach may or may not succeed depending upon the equation of the overall group or the community and their commitment and desire to be closer to the truth. Thus, for my readers who are already walking on this path I congratulate all of them. Those who are not and still wondering whether to or not I wish them all the best for their future endeavors and journey in the search of truth. May the God be your Guru and visit you in a human form to lead you all towards the truth as **"Guru Brahma Guru Vishnu Guru Maheshwara"** & with these notes I would like to close this chapter and continue our journey toward the next topic.

9. Moksha or Liberation

The **Advaitya** tradition considers moksha achievable by removing avidya (ignorance). **Moksha** is seen as a final release from illusion, and through knowledge (Anubhav) of one's own fundamental nature, which is Sat-Chit-Ananda. Advaitya holds there is no being/non-being distinction between Atman, Brahman, and Paramatma. The knowledge of Brahman leads to moksha, where Brahman is described as that which is the origin and end of all things, the universal principle behind and at source of everything that exists, consciousness that pervades everything and everyone. **Advaitya** Vedanta emphasizes Jnana Yoga as the means of achieving moksha. Bliss, claims this school, is the fruit of knowledge (vidya) and work (karma).

The **Dvaityavad** (dualism) traditions define moksha as the loving, eternal union with God (Vishnu) and considered the highest perfection of existence. **Dvaityavad** schools suggest every soul encounters liberation differently. Dualist schools (e.g. Vaishnava) see God as the object of love, for example, a personified monotheistic conception of Shiva or Vishnu. By immersing oneself in the love of God, one's karmas slough off, one's illusions decay, and truth is lived. Both the worshiped and worshiper gradually lose their illusory sense of separation and only one beyond all names remains. This is salvation to dualist schools of Hinduism. **Dvaityavad** Vedanta emphasizes Bhakti Yoga as the means of achieving moksha.

Among the **Samkhya** Yoga and Vedanta schools of Hinduism, liberation and freedom reached within one's life is referred to as jivanmukti, and the individual who has experienced this state is called jivanmukta (self-realized person). Dozens of Upanishads, including those from middle Upanishadic period, mention or describe the state of liberation, jivanmukti. Some contrast jivanmukti with videhamukti (moksha from samsara after death). **Jivanmukti** is a state that transforms the nature, attributes, and behaviors of an individual, claim these ancient texts of Hindu philosophy. For example, according to Naradaparivrajaka Upanishad, the liberated individual shows attributes such as:

- *He is not bothered by disrespect and endures cruel words, treats others with respect regardless of how others treat him*

- *When confronted by an angry person he does not return anger, instead replies with soft and kind words*

- *Even if tortured, he speaks and trusts the truth*

- *He does not crave for blessings or expect praise from others*

- *He never injures or harms any life or being (ahimsa), he is intent in the welfare of all beings*

- *He is as comfortable being alone as in the presence of others*

- *He is as comfortable with a bowl, at the foot of a tree in tattered robe without help, as when he is in a mithuna (union of mendicants), grama (village) and nagara (city)*

- *He doesn't care about or wear ṣikha (tuft of hair on the back of head for religious reasons), nor the holy thread across his body. To him, knowledge is śikha, knowledge is the holy thread, knowledge alone is supreme. Outer appearances and rituals do not matter to him, only knowledge matters.*

- *For him there is no invocation nor dismissal of deities, no mantra nor non-mantra, no prostrations nor worship of gods, goddess or ancestors, nothing other than knowledge of Self.*

- *He is humble, high-spirited, of clear and steady mind, straightforward, compassionate, patient, indifferent, courageous, speaks firmly and with sweet words.*

- *When a Jivanmukta dies he achieves Paramukti and becomes a Paramukta. Jivanmukta experience enlightenment and liberation while alive and after death i.e., after becoming Paramukta, while Videhmukta experiences enlightenment and liberation only after death.*

The pursuit for eternal truth ends at Moksha. The Vedas, Vedanta and the Vedanga all agree to this fact. The pursuit to eternal truth in a life are divided into four parts-**Dharma, Artha, Kama & Moksha**.

- **Dharma**- The wheel of **Dharma** rotates on righteousness and the discharge of worldly duties through the mode of righteousness. **Dharma** is Sattvic in nature. **Dharma** is the code of conduct embedded in the human DNA. **Dharma** is the inner voice of God or the conscience that speaks when we do something wrong, sinful & disgraceful and asks us to refrain from it.

135

- **Artha**- Is the pursuit of the meaning of life. At a superficial level of consciousness this stands at the pursuit of wealth, resources & respect and distributing them among the society. However as one realizes that the true wealth and respect comes from the rightful discharge of duties & helping serve the community and the world the material form of **Artha** which is a reward of our services transforms completely into its spiritual form and we understand the true purpose of our life. Our pursuit for Mother **Lakshmi** ends at Lord **Shri Vishnu** when we attain the true **Artha** of Life which automatically leads to prosperity & happiness at the material realms of life. Artha is **Rajasic-Sattvic** in nature.

- **Kama**-Is the binding psychic force which ties us to this life & lives beyond. It's the main cause & the effect for which we take various forms and choose to pursue various materialistic desires and fulfill them. This pursuit ends up in agitating & creating ego which results in our separation from the Paramatma. The **Kama** is **Rajasic-Tamasic** in nature. If one understands the true nature of **Kama** and redirects it towards the **Paramatma** only then Moksha can be attained as then the Kama transforms to **Sattvic-Rajasic** in nature.

- **Moksha**- The search for the truth ends here. As one understands Moksha and practices it during his lifetime the person gets spiritually liberated from all the worldly liabilities. He walks on the path of **Dharma** to do only **Nishkam Karma**. As a result, he doesn't feel any pain or sufferings while discharging his duties. He treats the test of **success & failure** as one. He has already understood that the fruits of karma as seen in the form of **success & failure** etc. are in the hands of the Lord. He understands that happiness and sadness are the two faces of the same coin & the coin itself lies at the hands of the Lord. Hence instead of focusing on the faces of the coin he focuses on the eternal energy who is responsible for **tossing** the coin. Thus, a **Yogi** pursuing **Moksha** while watching a Pendulum will not focus on its **to & fro** motion, but on the string, which is tied up to a **fixed point.** This **fixed point** of the pendulum is the **Moksha** point. All the rest are caused by the illusion or **Maya** of the psychic force of **Gravity.**

Now, the attachment and detachment are the two aspects of **Moksha.** When we attach ourselves to something, we at the other hand detach ourselves from some other thing at the same time. By choosing to attach ourselves to the pursuit of truth we can detach ourselves from the **Maya. Rahu** and **Ketu** are born out of the churning of the cosmic etheric ocean and are the two aspects of **Moksha.**

Rahu is the attachment of the soul to this universe and is the karaka of our mortal desires. He is the agent between the earth and the heavens. He is the agent of mother **Mahamaya** and serves as a messenger communicating all our desires, thinking and aspirations to her. He is the magician, expert wizard his kingdom is our passion. He is the main karaka of the virtualization occurring in the fields of technology, research and drives the innovation & new ways of doing business which has transformed the wealth into digital money in today's world and has changed the definition of money into mere numbers. He is the reason for all inflations and is the universal conspirator who works offline tracking on our thinking process. All the wireless devices and technologies are under his domain control. At lower levels of consciousness Rahu generates obsession which in terms keeps us binding to our unfulfilled desires. At a superficial level of consciousness in astrology, he is the head of the demon **Swarbhanu**. However, at a realized advanced level of consciousness he is the demigod born from **Swarbhanu's** severed head by **Mohini** avatar of Shri Vishnu. Thus, his divine form of **Rahu** is one of the **Navagraha** and is worshipped in the temples.

Astronomically **Rahu** & **Ketu** are the two points where eclipses occur. Hence, they cannot be seen by our mortal eyes and they are two invisible psychic forces.

Ketu on the other hand is the detachment of the soul and shows us the past life patterns that needs transformation in the current life to go a step forward in the path of realization of **Moksha**. Ketu in the subconscious lower levels can generate fear out of ignorance and drives us towards attaining knowledge about the subject to get liberated from the magic or Charisma of Rahu. Ketu is our spiritual companion, our isolation, our meditation & if a native can understand the psychic signals of Ketu to overcome one's ignorance can rise very quickly above all worldly **Maya** or Illusion. He can feel the blessings of God through the path of renunciation and become successful in understanding the mysteries of the world and finally become liberated from all world delusions.

A **Yogi** interested in only spiritual pursuits must isolate himself from the world and retire in seclusion so that he doesn't increase his karmic backlogs by being in a materialistic profession to accumulate resources to satisfy his worldly needs. He must walk on the path of renunciation in pursuit of spiritual liberation and must sever all his ties with the materialistic world. In Order to do so he must discharge all his worldly liabilities and get ready to take up the life of a **Sanyasi** as soon he has taken care of his duties. In today's world there are **Ashramas** that gives refuge to people and has become shelters for homeless & hopeless people who has lost everything in their lives and has not tasted of materialistic success even after several attempts. Such people often serve the purpose of running these **Ashramas** and perform community services, however, **Moksha** is not guaranteed through their acquaintances. The route to **Moksha** is different and doesn't usually go through that direction alone. Indulging in community services is only preferable when someone chooses to be the **Guru** of a larger section of people and try to guide them modify their lifestyle and transform them towards spirituality. Such **Gurus** often appear to be magnetic & their communication will be very hypnotic in nature. This is because of **Rahu** which creates in them such majestic and charismatic magnetism that helps them to attract more public attention towards them. In their past lives these **Gurus** might have practiced **celibacy** and they had this desire of spreading their messages about God & spirituality. Thus, the universe conspires and give them entry into the world by entrusting them with the duty of changing the lives of millions. However, sometimes their different teaching methodologies and techniques creates confusion due to **Maya** among their disciples who often start thinking their **Guru** as absolute after their exit from the mortal world. These, various teachings & practices then often become a new religion among their followers. Such

139

religions at the end often become corrupted with the political desires of their leaders who forgets all their teachings of their Gurus and indulge in malpractices to fulfill their political ambitions. Such leaders lead their religion and community towards destruction as they prepare to conflict with other religions and expand their own beliefs and force it upon the others to accept them. History is witness to such conflicts that has often led to war in battle fields where one group or community is the aggressor & the other group is defending their beliefs and practices. Such wars are known as **Dharma Yuddhas**.

Thus, in such wars **Moksha** awaits the warriors from both the groups either the aggressor or the defender. Universe often chooses the victorious based on a long-term utility of a group & its believers, often the group that suits the demand of that time and understand to serve its purpose. If the Universe has plans to propagate the beliefs of the aggressors and gives them more time for sustainability and preserving their core practices the probability of their victory becomes more in comparison to the defenders.

The probability of victory depends on several factors that universe uses for comparisons between the two parties at conflict. If the universe wants the defenders to learn a lesson and prepare themselves for a greater conflict in the future, it will just probably not lead them towards complete annihilation. Thus, few people among the defenders will survive and they after having learnt the hard lessons of the truth of nature will lead to the foundation of evolution of their remaining community into a different race through the power of their transformation. They will then emerge as aggressors and rewrite the history of hunting back the once hunter. It's difficult to understand the demands of the time and the purpose of the Universe however it's all under the **Mahakal.** Hence, if a warrior worships **Mahakal** or **Shiva** he will be able to acquire the vision that can probably help him to understand the flow of time. Such warriors can often defend their groups and save them from complete annihilation in case of lesser probability of victory. These warriors either become immortals in the chapters of history or they become key witnesses & participators of rewriting of the history by emerging as victorious when the time favors them. An example of such a warrior is **Chhatrapati Shivaji Maharaj** who was an ardent devotee of Lord Shiva.

This is an unending game of the universe where a hunter becomes hunted and the hunted becomes hunter alternatively. Now a million-dollar question as soon as we take birth, we assume the position of discharging numerous responsibilities towards our family, our society, our community or our tribe, our nation and finally towards our world. So how does our **Vairagya** give us liberation from all these worldly responsibilities?

The answer has been given by Shri Krishna in Bhagvada Geetha in the theory of Karma Yoga by the following slokas *Sri-bhagavan uvaca sannyasah karma-yogas ca nihsreyasa-karav ubhau tayos tu karma-sannyasat karma-yogo visisyate.*

The meaning of the above slokas is that the Lord said: ***The renunciation of work and work in devotion are both good for liberation. But, of the two, work in devotional service is better than renunciation of works.*** Thus, Lord Krishna says that one acting neutrally to discharge his duties thinking of only Shri Krishna does them comfortable and through a state of complete consciousness that this world, its countries, its communities and all the people residing on

141

it stands on a platform of illusion created by the Lord.

The rising situations and the people acting on them just exists to make us feel that we are awake in a state of deep sleep which has left an impression on our mind and consciousness that drives us to believe that the alternate reality created by the Lord's Maya is the actual reality. Thus, a devotee acting in complete Krishna consciousness will be able to transcend this alternate reality as he will have thorough knowledge that he is acting under the influences of the **Shadripu** on the platform of this alternate reality of Maya.

I am trying to give a synonymous example from the computer science operating system concepts which explains the difference between the actual **Operating Systems Kernel** and a **Virtual Machine** operating on top of OS Kernels each managing its own set pf processes. This world is infact a perfect example of virtualization and is infact a **Virtual Machine Containers** operating with its own set of processes on top of the OS Kernel which is the actual platform of the Lord. Thus, a devotee acting completely in Krishna consciousness is aware of this truth and acts in good faith through devotional service of his karmas to Krishna. He is aware that his Karma of executing VM processes is managed by the Virtual Machine Platform & as soon as the process has finished its execution it will enter a dead state in the process lifecycle and the Virtual Machine will reclaim its allocated memory. By constantly engaging in this consciousness the individual process has become aware of the actual OS Kernel under which this VM is functional. Thus, Krishna consciousness is the state under which a User Process makes a **System Call** to the underlying OS. When a User Process makes a **System Call**, the process transitions to running in Kernel space. When the System call returns, the process transitions back to running in user space.

Krishna consciousness is possible when acting under Bhakti Yoga. Thus, it is guaranteed that acting in Krishna consciousness while discharging worldly duties is superior to renouncing of the Karma itself and has been clarified by Lord Shri Krishna himself in the earlier Sloka. Thus, if we explain through the concept of computer science synonymously again it becomes synonymous to the fact the Bhaktas are like **System Processes** operating under the OS Kernel which has the privileges of Operating even under the customized Virtual Machine User Spaces for some specific amount of time. The reason of choosing this synonymous example is the readers of this book who have idea about the computing & virtualization will be able to corelate this example to better understand the theory of **Moksha** in a scientific manner.

Mostly all human beings are engaged in endless battles of words from the time they learn to speak till the time they are finally silenced by the time itself. By doing that they try to prove their points and satisfy their ego that their perspective is correct. However, if we look at it wisely, we will find that there is no concrete perspective to look at this world as everything is volatile and is a complete illusion. Our eyesight let's take an example is an illusion itself as science explains that we see only those objects which reflects light. It is only by reflection that we, as well as most of the other objects in our physical world, can be seen. Optical Physics explains that frame by frame movement of pictures are perceived by the eyes as a movie. The ears similarly can hear only those sounds whose frequencies are within the audible range.

Hence what we see, hear, and perceive are finite and beyond this sense of perception lies the unseen, unexplored truth of infinity. We can only perceive what the universe wants us to perceive. Through our limited experiences in the sequence of consecutive births and rebirths we identify the common patterns that connects us in between various frames and realize that how often our habits are based on those common patterns. Our evolution of the soul is untracked and marks a scientific limitation of the progress of constantly evolving our inner nature. Its only through inner voices that we resolve such conflicts within and evolve as either a better or even a worst individual. These inner voices are therefore important to our existences and the nature of these voices determine the true nature & character of an individual.

These inner voices are therefore the voice of the soul, its aspirations, past patterns based on various experiences. Very few people can deny that they don't hear such voices. Our etheric manas is getting constantly churned by the inner Devas and the Danavas which results in both the good and the bad things to come out as an outcome of such a churning. Our Nadis are either enlightened by the light of the heavenly fire or burnt painfully by the same degenerated hellish fire of our own darker hellish desires. Life is worth living when our **Brahma Urja** enlightens and brightens up our soul like a sun. The same life becomes miserable and painful when the same **Brahma Urja** becomes degenerated and hellish. Our whole life gets engulfed in the burning fire of hell. Thus, each **Brahma Urja** has the capability to transform the individual into divine or demoniac natures depending upon the resident individual and its purpose of existence. The knowledge of the science of **Brahma Vidya** is thus essential to manage the transcendence of the residing **Brahma Urja** and transform it to divine nature. **Moksha** operates

144

completely on that plane of the science of **Brahma Vidya** where the individual is no longer dependent on the limitations of the sense organs to perceive this universe.

Such individuals can perceive beyond the senses and can define what is undefined, can see what is unseen and can feel what cannot be felt by us. An individual who understands the science of **Brahma Vidya** & practices it is absolutely the one who has started preparing to be one and unite with the **Brahman**.

Thus, ends this chapter on **Moksha** after we have enabled the psychic forces within which can feel that unknown is just another term which simply refers to the limitations of the senses and all we want is freedom from such limitations.

10. Purusha and the Prakriti

The two most important components or concepts of the *Samkhya* Philosophy is **_Purusha_** and the **_Prakriti_**. Hence, to understand the perception of this psychic world we will have to understand the **Purusha** & from it the blossoming **Prakriti**. The Samkhya philosophy consists of the theory of Creation, Duality & Enumeration. **Kapil Muni** was the founder of this philosophy.

In the light of the computer science if we want to understand **Purusha** and the **Prakriti** principle then we will have to look at the object-oriented concept of the computer science. Analogically **Purusha** becomes the Class & **Prakriti** becomes the objects in the light of the object-oriented design of the computer science.

Now what was the reason for which I chose Samkhya Yoga? The reason for which I have chosen this wonderful philosophy of *Samkhya Yoga* is primarily because it is the only school of thought which identifies the dual aspects (**_Dvaityavad_**) of the psychic origination of the **Jivatmas** i.e. us.

Samkhya means **numbers** and we all know how **numbers** are important for all kinds of measurements in our human lives. **Samkhya Yoga** teaches us that this universe was born from infinity and that it will eventually dissolve in infinity. All other dimensions including three dimensions of space and one dimension of time are only relative. **Samkhya Yoga** believes in **the law of conservation of energy** as well as **_the law of conservation of matter_**.

Samkhya Yoga also identifies the theory of relativity of Einstein which says **E=mc2** where energy and mass are interconvertible. **Samkhya Yoga** says that light has dual nature a wave as well a particle nature (**_Dvaityavad_**). Thus, using **Samkhya Yoga** we can relate the **Sanatan** (Universal) cosmic science more to the modern classical Physics and the **Einsteinian** Quantum mechanics of **Photons**. Thus, **Samkhya Yoga** talks about zero from which this universe was born, it talks about negative infinity or eternity when there was absolutely nothing which led to the formation of zero & then **Samkhya Yoga** talks about the positive infinite where the universe started expanding from zero. Thus, **Samkhya Yoga** is the bridge that relates modern science to the ancient spiritual philosophies of the **Sanatan Dharma**.

Samkhya Yoga identifies the recently discovered "**God Particle**". Finding a Higgs-like boson validates much of how scientists believe the universe was formed. The media calls the Higgs boson the **God particle** because, according to the theory laid out by Scottish physicist **Peter Higgs** and others in 1964, it's the physical proof of an invisible, universe-wide field that gave mass to all matter right after the Big Bang, forcing particles to coalesce into stars, planets, and everything else. If the Higgs field, and Higgs boson, didn't exist, the dominant Standard Model of particle physics would be wrong. "There's no understating the significance" of this discovery: says Jeffrey Kluger at TIME. "*No Higgs, no mass; no mass, no you, me, or anything else.*"

Samkhya Yoga explains creation in an inclusive manner where the implicit manifests as explicit and the explicit transforms into the implicit through the psychic interactions of mass & energies, their interconversions, their eventual transformations into various *sub-atomic* forms. In the

Samkhya Yoga *Purusha* is the purest form of energy & is the most subtle form of the psychic consciousness called **Brahman** which we have discussed earlier. The universe is its **Prakriti** from which we all have been formed and will get ultimately dissolved unto and is thus the true nature of the **Purusha**.

Therefore, **Purusha** and **Prakriti** are two inseparables as **Purusha** is the energy form of the **Brahman** & **Prakriti** is the equivalent matter of the same. Thus, **Prakriti** is our mother one who nourishes us, whether it's the earth or our biological human mothers or even the cosmic mothers who nourishes us with the development of the various equivalent cosmic competencies. Therefore, our cosmic mothers are various forms of **Mother Shakti** by whose blessings the cosmic competencies reside within every individual human being as cosmic inner *Purusha* which we call *Purushartha*.

Prakriti is the matter and nature and it is the power of manifestation in all objects and holds all the three gunas under equilibrium. Thus, now scientifically it should be clearer how the **Brahman** as **Purusha** manifested as **Prakriti** in the form of this psychic universe. How we as human beings spiritually came into this universe, why do we get born & take several reincarnations, which cosmic realms does we enter after our earthly lifespan exhausts. Just like everything has an expiry date including our driving license, visa, Permanent Residency or Green Cards, home loans, insurance etc. our longevity or life span expires too. We then continue our eternal journey into this universe through renewal of our **Prakriti** in the form of reincarnation. Seldom do we realize that we all are eternal travelers and our stagnancy over some place, community, language, ancestors or national history & numerous reincarnations over a long relative period of time makes us feel & believe that we are human settlers. I realized this factor and the importance of **Samkhya Yoga** in our lives while I was living in **Silicon Valley** in US.

Now we will discuss in detail the **Purusha** and the **Prakriti** considering the Samkhya Yoga and what constitutes them. **Prakriti** has three primary constituents the three gunas **Sattva**-lucidity, **Rajas**-activity, **Tamas**-inertia. When the three gunas are in equilibrium, the universe remains unmanifested. But when this equilibrium is disturbed and becomes unbalanced, the material world unfolds into manifestation. An individual is a combination of **Purusha** and **Prakriti**. **Prakriti** includes twenty-four tattva & is always in state of equilibrium, the state of guan (sattva, rajas, tamas), the effect of it starts from buddhi that is evolved through Aham. Aham is caused through manas. Manas is evolved by five karmendriyan, five gyanedriyan and five mahabhuta. Buddhi, Aham, manas supports individual to perceive the situation i.e. internal (antahkaran) and 10 organs (gyanendriya and karmendrya) process the external (bahyakaran) situation.

This philosophy is depicted below in the form of a diagram.

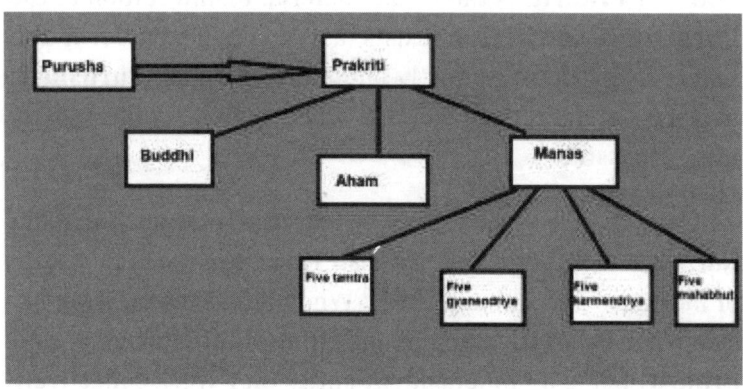

In the context of an individual **Purusha** is the soul/individual, **Prakriti** is the environment around that individual. **Prakriti** can exists around the individual as manifested or unmanifested. **Buddhi** is the intellect of the individual that influences its decision making. **Aham** or ego is the self-centric perception of the individual. **Manas** is the **Chitta** or the mind which contains the vast cosmic ocean of consciousness & emotions.

Five Tamtras	Five Gyanendriya	Five Karmendriyan	Five Mahabhuta
Form	Ear	Hand	Earth
Sound	Skin	Feet	Water
Smell	Eye	Speech	Air
Taste	Tongue	Excretion Organ	Space
Touch	Nose	Generation Organ	Fire

Both Purusha & Prakriti are the independent entities however **Prakriti** is the actual material manifestation of the **Purusha**. **Prakriti** can exists as unmanifested form too however that form is mostly limited to when the **Purusha** is in a state of deep **Yoga Needra** or sleep mode and is mostly inert & passive.

Its due to this factor that when the eternal **Purusha** Narayana is in **Yoga Needra** his **Prakriti** remains in a state of inertness and unmanifested. When he wakes up from his sleep his **Prakriti** starts manifesting. Both **Purusha and Prakriti** being an independent entity they work collectively

150

however as eternal consorts. **Samkhya** philosophy categorizes individual behavior in three gunas; **Sattva, Rajas, Tamas.**

One's nature and behavior constitute a complex interplay of all three gunas, lets see how. **Sattva** includes qualities of being optimistic, constructive, and upright. **Rajas** is active, urge, prospective either good or bad and **Tamas** is ignorance, inertia, destruction. According to Ayurveda three properties that exist in an individual are known as **Doṣha.** They are Vatta, Pitta & Kapha. The properties of **Doṣha** influence an individual's mind and body type through time, food, season, and other factors. Domination of different elements creates different action in the body and feelings in mind.

"By mastering the knowledge of these elements, we can try to understand through our wisdom of what is happening inside us and take regulatory measures to control & give right direction to our behaviors and worldly actions".

Let us try to understand this concept with the help of a simple example. *"**A known Smell enters through our nose and creates a stimulus in our nervous system by initiating the neurological chemicals that creates a bonded feeling about the perceptions of stability, peace & harmony of the known environment around us".***

Now if we try to relate this example with the various components of the Prakriti that were playing their role to make this happen we will find that *Smell is one of the five Tamtras, it entered through our nose which is one of the Five Gyanendriya & created neurological chemicals which is basically the earthly composition of the Five Mahabhuta which resulted in a stimulus which was precepted as an inertia of bondedness of the known which invoked the Doṣha of Kapha and was precepted as a mechanism of peace & stability which affected our mind & individual characteristics.*

. Modification in behavior comprises a change in environment. Gyanendriya (sense organ) is the means of entrance of feelings. Karmendriyan (action organ) is the means of expression. An individual perceives through Gyanendriya and acts through karmendriyan. This is explained scientifically below.

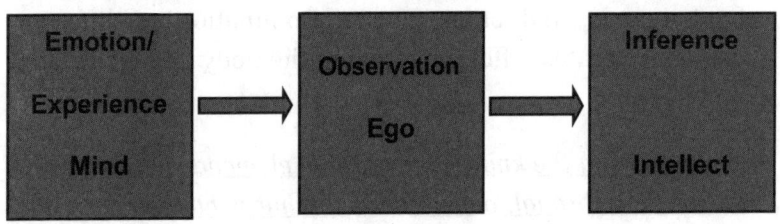

The above workflow impacts the decision-making abilities of an individual. As the **Prakriti** manifests into reality around the individual his perception about the world around him develops through his five senses. His characteristics & instincts are primarily three-fold and is exactly as above. Thus, the decision-making ability of an individual has been designed as a three-fold process.

By carefully evaluating the mind & the emotion a proper decision can be made by a Yogi if he acts through wisdom at the observation stage by minimizing his ego which can bring out the best of the intellect through the science of **Samkhya Yoga**. Thus, without the understanding & knowledge of the Purusha & the Prakriti a Yogi's spiritual pursuit is incomplete and his repeated attempts to achieve self-control and transformation might lead to failure. All the aspirants of spiritual path must therefore study the science of **Samkhya Yoga** and master the concepts of **gunas** to consciously design & develop the building blocks of a successful spiritual life.

This is certainly going to bring health, happiness & enormous joy into their lives by helping them design and engineer the daily habits which can make them highly successful by making the desired Prakriti to manifest into reality around their known world. Thus, this knowledge of the unknown is essential to build a known universe around us which is full of bliss, wisdom and happiness.

All my readers are therefore welcomed into this world of bliss which is the world of their true Prakriti. **Once they are completely aware of their Prakriti they can create miracles and can transform the unmanifested dream into manifested reality through the power of their desires.**

Many American authors use the above principle while writing self-improvement books for the commercial audiences, however the scientific concepts around them are all reengineered from **Samkhya Yoga & the Bhagvada Geetha.** For example, Rhonda Byrne & her best seller **The Secret** is one of those books whose core component has been based around the principles of **Samkhya Yoga.** Another example in the row is Stephen R Covey and his book, **The 7 Habits of Highly Effective People.**

In the modern world there are a lot of research that are conducted on developing leadership in the industry whether its Business, Engineering, Medical or any related commercial field.

However, the basic ingredients of all conducted research are filtered & obtained from the spiritual field. As these authors combine their personal experiences with the principles of **Samkhya Yoga,** they can relate their **Prakriti** to the **Rajasic Guna** of their commercial leadership qualities. The above relationship creates a strong wave of manifested reality around the readers & they too can relate to this relationship which ultimately leads to their inner transformation & further improvements in their habits and decision-making capabilities.

Thus, knowingly, or unknowingly we all are studying **Samkhya Yoga** & getting benefitted out of it such is the power & the capability of **Samkhya Yoga** for creating assets that can really change millions of lives and bring smiles into their faces. Once we rightly use **Samkhya Yoga** to create assets for the people around as we can emerge as true leaders and through the power of our convictions, we can create examples and motivate people to pursue the same to become successful in their pursuit of **self-realizations** which can bring out the best in them.

Thus, ends our discussion on Purusha & Prakriti and the principles of Samkhya Yoga and their benefits.

11. The Role of Astrology in Self Realization

Is Destiny Fixed For every individual? What is Karma and Nishkam Karma and what is Moksha? These are most queries on a searcher's mind.

The Slokas in the Bhagvada Geetha as said by Lord Shri Krishna says

"karmaṇy-evādhikāras te mā phaleṣhu kadāchana

mā karma-phala-hetur bhūr mā te saṅgo stvakarmaṇi"

Which means You have a right to perform your prescribed duties, but you are not entitled to the fruits of your actions. Never consider yourself to be the cause of the results of your activities, nor be attached to inaction.

Therefore, it is advisable that become a Karma Yogi and perform Nishkam Karma through Bhakti Yoga. Doing Karma is in our hands not deciding the fruits of it or its outcome either. Therefore, submit yourself to Shri Krishna's Bhakti and perform your duty. That process itself will decide your destiny once you engage in devotional service.

If one start reading Bhagvada Geetha mind will get clearer on destiny, action & inaction. One will rarely need to look for astrological consultancy or a remedy. The purpose of the astrology or an astrologer is not to make someone distract from his/her Karma and make that individual Karma Vimukh. An astrologer can predict events accurately when there is god's grace upon that astrologer.

With God's grace astrologer's third eye chakra awakens and his intuitive & meditative approach towards cosmic entities considering them as Gurus help an astrologer to predict some events in someone's life. So, there is nothing to feel delighted or disappointed when you see someone's horoscope and unfold the secrets of the individual's current life and his past lives.

All the Karmas are linked in chain reaction and triggers another chain of events. **Yes, the destiny and its direction are fixed.**

But this direct answer and how to handle the direction of destiny has been answered very beautifully and mysteriously by Lord Shri Krishna in Bhagvada Geetha when his dearest Friend Arjuna asks the same question.

Arjuna asks:

"Arjuna uvaca jyayasi cet karmanas te mata buddhir janardana tat kim karmani ghore mam niyojayasi kesava"

which means Arjuna said: O Janardana, O Kesava, why do You urge me to engage in this ghastly warfare, if You think that intelligence is better than fruitive work?

Krishna responded to Arjuna as in the below sloka:

"sri-bhagavan uvaca loke 'smin dvi-vidha nistha pura prokta mayanagha jnana-yogena sankhyanam karma-yogena yoginam".

This means The Blessed Lord said: O sinless Arjuna, I have already explained that there are two classes of men who realize the Self. Some are inclined to understand Him by empirical, philosophical speculation, and others are inclined to know Him by devotional work.

Shri Krishna further says:

"na karmanam anarambhan naiskarmyam puruso 'snute na ca sannyasanad eva siddhim samadhigacchati"

Which means not by merely abstaining from work can one achieve freedom from reaction, nor by renunciation alone can one attain perfection.

Shri Krishna further goes on and adds:

"na hi kascit ksanam api jatu tisthaty akarma-krt karyate hy avasah karma sarvah prakrti-jair gunaih".

This means that all men are forced to act helplessly according to the impulses born of the modes of material nature; therefore no one can refrain from doing something, not even for a moment.

Shri Krishna then instructs & reveals the truth mysteriously by saying:

"karmendriyani samyamya ya aste manasa smaran indriyarthan vimudhatma mithyacarah sa ucyate".

Which means One who restrains the senses and organs of action, but whose mind dwells on sense objects, certainly deludes himself and is called a pretender.

Shri Krishna then adds how to manage the Karma

"yas tv indriyani manasa niyamyarabhate arjuna karmendriyaih karma-yogam asaktah sa visisyate"

Which means on the other hand, he who controls the senses

by the mind and engages his active organs in works of devotion, without attachment, is by far superior. Shri Krishna then advises Arjuna and prescribes the solution:

"niyatam kuru karma tvam karma jyayo hy akarmanah sarira-yatrapi ca te na prasiddhyed akarmanah".

Which means perform your prescribed duty, for action is better than inaction. A man cannot even maintain his physical body without work. He adds further to it and says:

"yajnarthat karmano 'nyatra loko 'yam karma-bandhanah tad-artham karma kaunteya"mukta-sangah samacara".

Which means work done as a sacrifice for Visnu has to be performed, otherwise work binds one to this material world. Therefore, O son of Kunti, perform your prescribed duties for his satisfaction, and in that way, you will always remain unattached and free from bondage.

Thus, at the beginning of this chapter the universal law of Karma & how to manage it is crystal clear. However, when individuals face obstacles in their life to accomplish their desired goals and face challenges while performing the required action, they often loose track of the universal law of Karma and can visit astrology to redirect them back to the right track by analyzing into their specific individual problems to find a right solution. This is again another Karma of finding the right direction of Karma through the eyes of Veda known as **Jyotish** or Astrology. Thus, the formula of **Jyoti + Ish= Jyotish** rightfully explains astrology as the divine light of god.

This chapter emphasizes importance to understand few key

astrological & astronomical concepts to figure out the role of astrology in self realization and working through a Karmic problem to find a transformative solution to the Karma.

The subject of astrology itself has been descended from renowned sages like Bhrigu Parashar, Vyasa to their disciples like sage Jaimini. Indian Astrology is more than ten thousand years old and is part of the Vedanga. The study of the cosmic occurrences through their astronomical observations & their relationship to the terrestrial events have been established through astrology. It's an astronomical & statistical science and are divided into six primary branches as below:

➤ Gola: Positional astronomy

➤ Ganita: Mathematical calculations to find Gola

➤ Jataka: Natal astrology

➤ Prasna: Answering question based on the time it is asked

➤ Muhurta: Auspicious time to start anything

➤ Nimitta: Omens and portents

Much knowledge & wisdom has been lost through the tide of time & subsequent foreign invasions of India. However modern-day scholars like late **Prof Shri B.V Raman & Prof. Shri K.S. Krishnamurti** have been able to preserve the wisdom of the ages and has given a hope to the younger generations to continue their research on Vedic astrology.

There has been deliberate attempts to deny & suppress the truth behind Vedic astrology during medieval times from foreign rulers & the foreigners however the pursuit of occult knowledge, mysticism and the truth has never failed the wisdom of the curious Indian minds which has been blessed by their ancestors and the ancient sages.

Indian Astrology is broadly classified into twelve zodiacs known as rasis; nine planets known as grahas & 27 constellations known as nakshatras.

Mythologically these 27 nakshatras are related to the 27 daughters of Daksha married to Chandra or Moon. The nine planets are Sun, Moon, Jupiter, Saturn, Venus, Mercury, Rahu & Ketu. Out of the nine planets Rahu & Ketu are not luminaries they are rather shadowy planets and represents astronomically the points where eclipse occur. The rulership of the twelve zodiacs are divided among the seven planets. The rulership of the 27 constellations are divided among the nine planets and each nakshatra has their ruling deity. Life cycle of Jivatmas born on earth in any form human or animal falls under the domain of the Navagraha. Even when Paramatma takes incarnation on this earth as a conditioned soul or avatar his karmic manifestations falls under the jurisdiction of the Navagraha. Navagraha are the cosmic manifestations of the supreme soul on the solar plane and their job is to provide conditioned Karmic results to an individual through several incarnations of birth and rebirth. Jupiter & Venus are presided over by the Gurus Brihaspati & Shukra. Sun & Moon are presided over by the luminaries Surya & Chandra. Mars & Mercury are presided over by Mangal & Buddha Deva. Saturn is presided over by Shani Deva the protector of justice, masses & their rights. Rahu & Ketu are the distractors and acts as consultants between the Navagraha.

Each of this Grahas are our earthly Gurus and they have

something special to teach to us during their phases on our lives. These phases astrologically are known as Vimshottari Dashas. Human life span is considered 120 years and the Dasha System is divided among the nine planets accordingly. For example, Jupiter Dasha runs for sixteen years and during this the individual will be conditioned to Karma under Jupiter's guidance. Jupiter rules over wisdom, Dharma & expansion of it. Therefore, During Jupiter's phase, the individual's Karmic direction may get activated towards Dharmic scriptures, their studies and awakening the inner wisdom through those studies. The individual may also learn astrology and get motivated to become a healer.

Each horoscope is divided into twelve houses and each house rules over specific attributes, people, and places of our lives. The ascendant or the first house is the rising sign of the horizon and represents the individual itself. Its Nakshatra and the location of the lord of the ascendant can tell us the karmic direction of the evolution of the individual soul. Similarly, the location of the Moon in the birth chart and its nakshatra can tell us about the development of the consciousness of the soul and its direction of evolution. Moon is the mind and the emotion of the individual. The position and aspects of Saturn in the birth chart shows us the liabilities, commitments, social status, Karmic backlogs and the areas of efforts, disciplines, and organizational abilities of the individual. The location of the Gurus in the horoscope shows the areas of Karmic enlightenments, wisdom, sense of beauty, long term vision & the ability to guide for an individual. The location of Mercury shows the area of intelligence whereas the location of Mars & its aspects shows the areas where the individual has proactive Karmic abilities, sportsmanship & leadership capabilities. The location of the Sun talk about the Karmic progress of the soul and the divine purpose of its reincarnation. Rahu & Ketu position shows our desires for which we have reincarnated on this earth and the direction through which we may renounce our Karma through sequences of attachments and detachments. Rahu is our desire, our attachment & obsession, our cause to enter this world whereas Ketu is our renunciation, our detachments & withdrawal, our inner effect to exit this world. Rahu and Ketu therefore are two psychic forces which always works together however in opposite directions just like the two poles of a magnet. All technological innovations & their implementation are under Rahu's domain whereas their continuous improvements and the efforts of minimizing their cons are under Ketu's domain.

The twelve zodiac signs in each of the twelve houses in a native's chart correspond to circumstances and the houses are the domains under which these circumstances will manifest. Since each planet rules over these zodiacs all the circumstances that manifest in our lives are brought about by them, their placements in different signs shows our abilities to react & manage in those circumstances and their placements in the nakshatras shows how we are going to evolve through our karmic experiences. The longitude of the planets in the zodiacs shows their avasthas or the states of readiness and how experienced they are to manage those circumstances in our lives. For example, a Graha in awakened state will engage and react more actively to a situation than a Graha in sleeping state. Grahas which are yet to mature occupy lesser longitudes than Grahas which are already Karmically matured. Therefore, the direction of Dharma, Artha, Kama & Moksha are fixed and conditioned under the Navagraha & can be studied through their birth charts.

All the righteous karmas are stored by the Navagraha corresponding to their domains & they update our individual accounts with them through our progress of incarnations. These are reflected in the form of Raj Yogas in the birth charts. During the Dasha of these Yoga forming Planets in the current birth we enjoy the fruits of those good karma which renders comforts in our lives. Similarly, the sins committed in the past lives are also updated by Navagraha for our accounts and the data reflects as Doṣha in our birth charts. While taking an incarnation we chose the purpose of our birth and our karmic desires decides the port of entry and exit from this world. Therefore, the divine right gives us an opportunity to decide our Lagna or the ascendant. We therefore get the right to decide where, how & why to reincarnate and take birth. After we are born how to enjoy the fruits of the Karma, where to enjoy it, whether we are going to enjoy it or not are all decide the Navagraha. The Moon or the mind is the eye of the soul through which we see this world and develop our consciousness. While the position of the ascendant shows the actual physical manifestation of the reality around us, the position of the moon and shows how we will see that reality and feel it. At lower levels of consciousness these experiences are felt as emotions which are governed by Moon. However, at higher levels of consciousness these experiences are felt as Yogic Self Realizations where we are becoming more aware of the cosmic consequences of our Karmas & how to purify them to achieve cosmic perfections which drives our spiritual growth and cosmic awareness.

Thus, astrology is a scientific tool to monitor, enhance & grow our spiritual awareness. However, as I mentioned at the beginning of this chapter, we only get to decide to do the karma, where and how to enjoy its fruits are not in our control. The Moon nakshatra in the birth chart talks about the direction & timing of the Dashas which will decide the fruits of the karma according to the Yogas formed by the planets in the birth charts. As those Dasha or phase of the planets progresses in sequences each Yoga is activated accordingly. When someone studies astrology these concepts become clearer and the mathematics and the logic behind Dasha systems can be accurately explained with reference to the life cycle of an individual by an astrologer whose third eye chakra is awake.

Now we will discuss few of the key astrological concepts behind Karmic Grahas like Saturn, Rahu, Ketu, Jupiter & Venus which can help in understanding how they function. We will also discuss about the three dusthana houses 6,8,12 and their significances in deciding the fruits of Karma of our lives.

We will begin with the discussion of the chief planet which is the divine judge of our karmas and always impartially delivers the fruits of them. Saturn is the protector of justice, individual rights, purification of the soul & defines our ability to organize, put efforts & emphasize discipline & much needed restrictions on our lives. Saturn defines the highest level of Karma Yoga in the material life and therefore his Dasha comes after Jupiter Dasha where he tests our abilities to implement the divine wisdom and principles of Jupiter at root level in our earthly lives which is full of challenges, struggles & limitations. Jupiter therefore becomes debilitated at the earthly sign of Capricorn which is the house of Karma Yoga. Therefore, Karma Yoga takes off from the point where Gyan Yoga becomes lowest. Karma is therefore the key to awaken wisdom on the earthly plane, as we work through it and get to manage it through complex

Karmic implementations the Karma Yoga reaches its peak where Saturn becomes exalted at Libra the sign of balance. Libra is ruled by Venus which becomes exalted at Pisces which is again the sign of Jupiter. Venus being our compassion balances our Karma by combining with Dharma & Gyan. Therefore, Venus is the balance between Jupiter & Saturn. Therefore, if we combine Karma with compassion and perform conscious active compassionate Karma through our dedicated services to Lord Shri Krishna our Karma gets the required direction as explained in the beginning of this chapter.

Rahu & Ketu on the other hand are the distractors as they act on our desires, attachments, fantasies and churn them rigorously which can produce an ocean of cosmic tempest inside us. Since they were born from Samudra manthan they develop an inertia inside the native to make them aware of their presence through constant churning of their inner primordial ocean. At lower levels of consciousness, they can really test the native by chasing him to lowest levels of the residual mortal desires inside them. At highest levels of consciousness if the direction of the desire of the native is inclined towards the divine, they can really test the dedication through constantly posing distractions & obstacles to hamper the focus, concentration & attention of the native. However, since Rahu & Ketu resides at the Brahma Loka & works under divine instructions, they can only cause sufferings or pains related to residual Rajas Guna in our inner consciousness. Sometimes they can cause good amount of suffering and pains to the Yogi if the permissible planets like Jupiter, Venus allows them to for testing the consistency & the strength of constitution. Rahu rules over all kinds of thieves, smugglers, alcohol, drugs & all forms of potent & fatal Venom. Therefore, among all the Navagraha

165

Rahu can render the highest form of pain to native's life and make his life poisonous and vile. Ketu on the other hand can cause remorse and can motivate the native negatively at lowest levels of consciousness to release the pain and the poison through renunciation of the life which can cause suicidal tendencies of withdrawal in the individual.

If Rahu & Ketu afflicts an individual's birth chart, they are bound to test the individual's patience & faith on the divine. If only the individual transforms their desire and directs it to the almighty lord shri Krishna only then healing can be done by praying to Lord Hanuman to rescue the native from the fangs of mysterious & foggy karmic cycles of Rahu & Ketu. **Kalsarpa Yoga** or the deadly Serpent Yoga formed by all the hemmed planets between Rahu & Ketu in a horoscope thus is capable of slowly creating a cloud of deception in the mind of the native & slowly drag & drown his consciousness in a deadly poisonous marshy land where they will trap the soul in an unending course of hellish suffering while they keep on repeating the same mistakes and gradually loses & forgets all lessons of purification. Rahu & Ketu which are the dragon's head & tail works together like a deadly predator snake trapping & hunting the individual with a **Kalsarpa Yoga** in their horoscope which eventually becomes the destiny of the native.

However, the positive effects of Rahu & Ketu are there too. They amplify the quality of the signs or the planets with which they are placed and aspects upon. Rahu & Ketu can take notorious & magical tests with the permission of the cohost, occupant and test our divine faith and Yogic merits & provide enlightenment before the cohost, occupant planets decide to provide the results of the Raj Yoga to the native. Rahu & Ketu can form brilliant Raj Yogas sometimes which are sometimes quite difficult to decipher by an astrologer. The rise of the native through this Raj Yogas surprises everyone around him such are the magical effects of those Raj Yogas.

As I was writing this chapter the world was passing through a pandemic of COVID-19. I studied the mundane astrologically and found how **Kalsarpa Yoga** can give the results of a deadly pandemic. Below is my analysis

"A great epidemic has come upon mankind and it all started when 6 planets were there in one Rashi together. This position was perfect for a **Kalsarpa Yoga**. Kal means deadly and Sarpa means serpent. It's the deadliest curse of the serpent or the Nagas which has come upon us. This planetary position happens only once in 20 years. Sun is our immunity and vital energy, and 3rd house is our ability to implement that vital energy in the form of our resistance.

Rahu's exalted position in the 3rd house of Gemini had not only given it enough strength to weaken our resistance but had also given it opportunity to disguise as Mercury which also rules over 6th House of diseases.

Rahu was just waiting for the dawn of Solar eclipse so that it can start its mysterious Karma and inject the epidemic.

Rahu's aspect on Jupiter in Sagittarius formed the needed Guru Chandal Yoga and Rahu will teach us the practical rules of this world however it will do its work of Chandala.

It will take us to Samsans and make us realize that our near and dear ones will be suffering from diseases and may even die, and we might have to suffer the same fate or live on their left over assets.

There will be many conspiracy theories around its origin however the fact and explanation will remain mysterious".

Now we will be discussing briefly about the dusthana houses 6,8,12 in astrology and at the end we will talk about retrograde planets and their significances in astrology for self-realization.

Firsts we will talk about the most difficult of the dusthana houses i.e., the 8th house, which is the house of longevity, transformation, taxes, obstacles, chronic diseases, taboos, legacies & inheritances. It's also the house of occult & paranormal connections in astrology. Deep down its roots 8th house is the house of Brahma Vidya and Sadhanas. It's a house of mysticism and mysteriously transforms our lives to help us motivate towards the path of Brahma Vidya. Once a Yogi realizes the importance of this moksha house his cosmic awareness starts and will lead towards continued realization of the world beyond this mortal eyes. He will be able to visualize the universe & the universes beyond.

Next comes is the 6th house, which is the house of health, lifestyle, services, competitors & holds the key to our happiness. It is also the house of curable diseases. Therefore, a string 6th house and lord are essential to render our services and contributions to this universe as well as follow a healthy lifestyle which holds the key to our happiness. This house is the Artha house which means managing this house successfully adds meaning to our lives as well as adds value through our services and contributions to the society.

Finally comes the 12th house which is the house of the final liberation or Moksha and signifies our essential expenditures, foreign residence, life in ashrams and isolated places like imprisonment, hospitals etc. Managing this house gives liberation from the current life through spiritual self-realizations & cosmic awareness.

Let us now understand the significance of retrograde planets in astrology. A retrograde planet means unfinished business of past life and depending on its karaka and placement shows what are the areas we will have to rework in this life to complete our Karma.

Therefore, Jupiter retrograde will show that we have unfinished business in religion, philosophy, wisdom & pursuit of dharma. Saturn retrograde will show unfinished karmic backlog in the areas of duties & commitments, efforts, disciplines & administrations. Mercury retrograde will show unfinished intellectual pursuits & Mars retrograde will show unfinished leadership pursuits. Venus retrograde shows unfinished business around luxuries, sensuality & aesthetic pursuits. Sun & Moon are never retrograde whereas Rahu and Ketu are always retrograde.

Thus, at the end of this chapter we are able to understand how astrology is helpful not only at an individual level, but also mundane astrology can help us find out the direction of karma at a collective level and help us analyze the collective karma and its destiny for a group, community, country. We can always create a horoscope for a group, or a country based on their date of creation, time & place of creation and analyze their karmic transformations, phases of it and the direction of the karma.

12.   Self -Realization & The Role of Kundalini

Kundalini is the Primordial cosmic energy located at the base of the spine. We have already discussed about the chakras and the chakra system. However the significance of Kundalini with respect to self-realization and the inner awakening is a distinct topic and has to be discussed in detail which will create an understanding on why our kundalini awakens, what are the circumstances that kundalini can manifest & why Kundalini management is important in our lives.

Invoking the Kundalini is like the call of the wild and the temptation becomes inevitable especially with the company of a Guru. Most of the Indian Gurus or Healers in the western world try this technique only the terminologies are different. Some calls it **Chakra Healing** whereas the others call it **Kundalini Sadhana**. These healing techniques have become quite popular over these years.

The physical practices of yoga consist of two parts – viz **Mudras & Asanas**. Mudras are various gestures of the hand which technically speaking are used to regulate the flow of cosmic energies inside the astral body. Each Mudra or a gesture symbolizes a specific form of an energy like Vishnu, Garuda, or Kundalini.

By practicing **Mudras**, we are awakening these energies into our astral body. **Mudras** are generally practiced along side **Asanas** followed by the science of breathing known as **Pranayama**. Each **Asana** is a symbolic physical representation of an object or technique. Thereby continuously practicing **Asanas** a Yogi integrates with the energy of the invoked object or a technique.

As given by **Darwin** the science of evolution states that species constantly evolve through a continuous process of transformation of their daily habits which induces permanent changes in them. The science of **Yoga** incorporates this theory and a normal human being slowly evolves as a Yogi by constantly & consciously invoking changes by integrating with specific energy patterns that brings permanent changes into their consciousness & lives. Thus, Yogis are a completely different species of human beings who evolve because of continuous Yogic practices.

With the evolution of these Yogis new states of evolution of the inner cosmic realties emerge. The role of kundalini here in shaping the Yogi becomes more important. Throughout the evolution process Kundalini plays the key role. Once the kundalini is invoked through the science of breathing there is no escape. Life becomes a complete playground of the **Samudra Manthan** or the churning of the cosmic energy ocean.

Therefore, to understand what the results kundalini will bring into our lives & in which sequence, it's important to understand the story of **Samudra Manthan** and what was the outcome of it, what were the various things that came up as a result of **Samudra Manthan** and how they were distributed. Whenever kundalini is activated it will start the process of the inner **Samudra Manthan.**

Whenever Kundalini awakens it will create constant inner conflict of **immortality** v/s **reincarnation**. Therefore, its important to understand who initiated **Samudra Manthan** & why. Samudra Manthan was proposed by **Shri Vishnu** &

implemented by **Lord Indra** so that the Devas can drink nectar and become immortals. This was in response to the Sanjeevani Mantra given to **Shukracharya** the Guru of the **Danavas** by **Lord Shiva** which could render them the status of immortality by bringing them back from death.

The **Danavas** had started killing the **Devas** which lowered their numbers and disbalanced the power equation in the universe. **Shri Vishnu** therefore proposed **Lord Indra** to initiate **Samudra Manthan** to restore the lost glory of the **Devas** due to a curse of Sage Durvasa & preserve **Dharma**. Lord Indra had to accomplish this difficult task by partnering with their enemies i.e. the **Danavas**. Therefore, Samudra Manthan or the cosmic churning is the story of **immortality** v/s **reincarnation** & why only the righteous or the **Devas** are only enlightened for **immortality** and the rest for only **reincarnation** to honor the laws of this universe created by **Lord Brahma**.

The reason for our human birth is primarily associated with **Lord Brahma**. **Brahma** created the heavens to motivate the ordinary human beings to pursue the desire or **Kama** of attaining the highest form of the material bliss in the form of the seven heavens. We as earthly human beings do the groundwork here at the earthly plane of seven earth. The earthly sphere is again seven layered or seven earth and exists in the form of seven continents. By accumulating **Punya** or good karma we can enjoy the highest form of material bliss i.e., heavens. The process of accumulating Punya is known as **Dharma** or righteousness. Therefore, when we follow the path of **Dharma,** we receive the rewards in the form of **Artha** which adds meaning and values to our life.

These **Artha** can be divine or material. **Material Artha** provides enjoyment and helps to fulfill our earthly liabilities through currencies, profits, movable & immovables properties & possessions. Divine **Artha** gets accumulated as **Punya** and increases our lifespan and longevities. Once an enlightened human being realizes the above truth, he doesn't attach himself to his **Kama**. His life becomes a **yagna** or a sacrifice where he sacrifices his **Kama** and purifies & transforms it to attain **Moksha** or liberation. Whatever he does he considers it as the will of the God, and he surrenders himself to the cause with full faith. Those who are aspirants of Heavens & doesn't believe in the above process of following **Dharma** & tries to forcibly hijack & enjoy the material benefits of the Heavens descends and takes birth into the seven lower worlds of **Patala**. They are known as **Asuras** or **Danavas** and they represent the sinners and the evil.

Once we exhaust our longevity and attain death through either disease or any other cause fixed by the destiny according to the laws of our Karma our material bodies dissolve into the five **mahabhuta**.

Our souls go to **Yama Loka,** the land of dead for either rebirth or heavenly ascent.

Those who are aspirants of the heaven and are sinners therefore descend into the fires of the hell from the **Yama Loka**. A soul is only entitled to enter the portal of heaven if it's pure. Therefore, aspirants of the heaven who are sinners descend into the fires of hell so that they are purified of their sins. They are then reincarnated into either the seven-fold earth or the seven-fold patala. By taking rebirth these souls fall under the domain of the **Navagraha** or the nine astrological cosmic planets. Thereafter they suffer the fruits of their Karma on this seven-fold earth or the seven-fold lower worlds.

The same form of cosmic fire if heavenly doesn't burn one as the already purified beings are like ashes which cannot be further burned, whereas the hellish fire can burn and cause great suffering if one descends into hell.

The process of **Samudra Manthan** was undertaken with three important tools-

1. The base or the **Mount Mandarachal** which physically represents our spinal cord.

2. The **Rajju** or the rope in the form of a coiled snake or **Naga** called **Nagaraj   Vasuki** which represents our **Kundalini Shakti.**

3. The crown or the root of **Kurma** or **tortoise** where the base was supported. This was **Shri Vishnu** himself represented by our root chakra or **Muladhara**. The **Muladhara** represents our sense of safety & security on this earth as already discussed.

The actors acting on these three cosmic tools are the **Devas** and the **Danavas** that represents the cosmic prayers v/s evil temptations in our four-fold eternal cosmic life viz. **Dharma, Artha, Kama** & **Moksha**. Once we understand these concepts through the study of comparative cosmology the rest i.e. the outcome of the manthan and its effect on our lives and in which sequence becomes very clear. We understand in this process that where do we stand in the progress of the reality of **immortality** v/s **reincarnation**.

Therefore, the kundalini either automatically awakens in the lifetime of an individual specially if astrologically the native passes through a Dasha of **Rahu** and the Antardasha of **Venus**. **Rahu & Ketu** were born out of the **Samudra Manthan** & therefore during their Dasha it becomes important for them to make us realize the reason of their birth and their cosmic connections to us.

Therefore, **Rahu** creates temptation and activates the Kundalini during **Shukra** Antardasha who the primary cause was due to which **Samudra Manthan** was initiated by **Lord Vishnu**. After **Rahu** Dasha comes Jupiter Dasha where you get a Guru who tells you how to manage your awakened **Kundalini** wisely so that you can reap the benefits of the emerging nectar that could result out of the churning process. The Guru can be in human form or the native can accept to act directly under the guidance of any Divine Guru or his **Aradhya**. For example, **Rama Krishna Paramhans** accepted to act under the guidance of **mother goddess Kali** as his Guru.

Now its upto the native to act wisely under guidance from the Guru and choose reincarnation after the knowledge of the **Seven Chakras** or the **Seven Heavens** & the **Moksha** or the native can choose to act in temptation without a Guru & may try to steal the nectar in trying to become an immortal. He might even get the temporary status of immortality like **Rahu** & **Ketu** and may even ascend to **Brahma Loka** however Lord **Vishnu** will make sure through his beautiful **Sudarshan** wheel or chakra of time that he separates such a native into two parts and make them unwanted, an outcaste and eternal wanderer before such natives becomes enlightened under the strict guidance of **Brahma**. Which means they will have to take rebirths and each of their incarnations will be partial like **Rahu** & **Ketu** and born out of the temptations where the simultaneous **psychic forces** of attraction & repulsion, attachment & detachments, intelligence & foolishness, Social Engagements & withdrawal will parallelly act together on these natives.

Immortality only comes at the cost of reincarnation and none including the **Devas** or the **Danavas** can become immortal beyond a **Kalpa**. **Lord Shiva** dissolves everything at the end of a **Kalpa** and then **Brahma** starts recreating the universe. Therefore, wisemen doesn't look for immortality as they are aware that immortality can sometimes become a curse and very painful like the examples of Mahabharata where **Bhisma**, **Ashwatthama** were cursed with immortality. The inner conflict of a human being however rises with the awakening of the **Kundalini** whose front side or the head is being dragged by the evil of the temptation or the **Danavas** & the latter part or the tail is being dragged by the mode of goodness, righteousness & faith represented by the **Devas**. Symbolically, Rahu therefore known as Dragon's head which represents the Kundalini under the control of the **Danavas** & Ketu as Dragon's tail which represents the part under the control of the **Devas**.

Therefore, whenever we introspect any truth the voices that drives the process is that of the temptation of the evil. Then at the later part comes the voice from the pure inner consciousness. This analogy is very important to understand the actual definition of the truth. For many individuals the meaning of the truth stands at a narratable story which can be legally constructable with the help of supporting evidence or claims and witnesses or testimonies in support of the constructed evidence. Often these truths are born out of conspiracies and joint ventures of a group whose mutual interests lies in deconstructing the actual truth which lies

176

hidden. Truth therefore stands apart from malice & manipulations and represents a stream of light among dominating presence of darkness. Truth always gives hope. Truth is therefore Shiva and always ensures the destruction of evil temptations.

Now whenever the Kundalini is awakened its first outcome coming out from the depths of the inner ocean of the cosmic consciousness is the **poison** which represents the toxicity of the **Kundalini**. Therefore, when the Kundalini of an ordinary man awakens, he first undergoes the tremendous pain of burning under the toxicity of this inner poison of consciousness. This toxic poison starts killing his inner demons like in the case of the **Samudra Manthan** where the poison from the fangs of the serpent Vasuki started destroying the **Danavas**. They paid for their foolish temptation of leading from the front. Therefore, the toxicity of Kundalini transforms into a sacrificial fire which starts vanquishing the inner demons of different evil temptations that lies on the surfaces of the cosmic ocean of consciousness.

Then appears the **Halahal** or the toxic poison of Karma from the inner depths of the cosmic ocean of consciousness which surfaces because of the churning of the ocean of consciousness due to Kundalini awakening. This poison is so potent that it can disturb the inner balance between both known and unknown as well as good and bad by destroying both good and bad habits that stands at the base of our existences. Just like the Halahal started killing the **Devas** and the **Danavas**. This is the truth or the **Shiva** and only by worshipping **Neelkanth Mahadeva** at this stage that such an individual can heal from the toxicity of his Karma which results out of his Kundalini awakening and inner churning of the cosmos consciousness. **Neelkanth Mahadeva** for such a Yogi can absorb all his **Karmic Halahal** and save him from burning this hellish poison which he generates out of the hellish toxicity of his accumulated past life Karmas. Sometimes an individual accumulates an entire ocean of Karmic toxicity and can drown and destroy himself while trying for Kundalini Yoga.

However, the lord is merciful and **Neelkanth Mahadeva** himself can take that pain by drinking his Karmic poison so that the aspirant can remain safe and continues his journey of enlightenment. Once the **Halahal** is neutralized one by one all the **Seven Chakras** awakens inside the Yogi which activates them sequentially. This inner awakening results in sequentially receiving the below benefits from each Chakras starting from the **Muladhara** till the Crown Chakra.

1. Sense of security, various competencies & the ability to lay foundation for a healthy living. Strong personality & leadership capabilities. Wealth generation.

2. Sensual accomplishment, Procreation & multiplication through child births.

3. Nutrition based diet and health regulation.

4. Healthy heart and compassionate feelings for others. Talent generation & retention.

5. Charming voice & ability to communicate effectively & positively. Wealth & asset retention.

6. Long term vision, good memory, and the ability to perceive and connect.

7. Psychic abilities to perceive beyond known and the power of conviction, truth, transformation & reformation

Now the **fourteen** emerging **Ratnas,** the results of the **Samudra Manthan** are given below and each of these has a deep meaning with respect to our existences.

1. **Lakshmi** or the goddess of wealth, fortune & prosperity who chose Vishnu as her consort.

2. **Apsaras** or divine beautiful women consorts who chose Gandharvas for companionship.

3. **Varuni** which includes all sorts of intoxicated drinks and were offered to the Danavas or the demons.

4. **Kamadhenu** or the nutritional cow which can fulfill any Kama or desire to pursuit any materialistic wish. It was claimed by the Devas and given to the sages.

5. **Airavat** or the royal elephant which was claimed by Lord Indra.

6. **Uchhashrava** or the seven headed horse offered to the demon king Bali.

7. **Kaustabha** the most valuable jewel and offered to Vishnu.

8. **Parijata** the divine tree that never wilts.

9. **Sharanga** the powerful bow offered to Vishnu.

10. **Kalpavriksha** the divine tree which can fulfill any desire. It was claimed by the Devas.

11. **Shankha** or the conch of Vishnu whose vibration

symbolizes victory.

12. **Chandra** the divine manas or Chitta or consciousness which was offered to Lord Shiva. It became part of Shiva's crown and Shiva thus came to be known as **Chandrasekhar Mahadeva**.

13. **Dhanvantri** the divine physician who can cure any disease.

14. The **Amrit** or the nectar of immortality is in the hands of **Dhanvantri**. He holds the secret to immortality.

When the Kundalini is therefore awakened it brings fourteen important aspects to the native's life corresponding to the fourteen **Ratnas**.

These aspects are:

1. Prosperity & ability to flourish with the help of wealth generation corresponding to **Lakshmi**.

2. Once wealth & prosperity accompanies the native it leads to the attraction & focus of beautiful women on him for companionship & enjoyments corresponding to the **Apsaras**.

3. Intoxication & consumption of alcoholic beverages for enjoyments then follow the pursuits of the native after he starts enjoying the company of the beautiful females. This is corresponding to **Varuni**.

4. Once the above desires for wealth, beautiful women & intoxications are fulfilled then the native wishes for real spiritual nourishments and pursues spiritual growth & nutrition. His search & quest for truth

begins. This is corresponding to **Kamdhenu** where he uses his wisdom to pursue righteousness in his life.

5. Once the pursuit of the **Dharma** begins the native receives the highest royal state or prestige in his life which carries the flag of the **Dharma** represented by **Airavat** or the royal elephant of the gods.

6. Once the native receives royal prestige, he starts performing charity of the highest forms. **Ashvamedha Yagna** or the sacrifice of the horse fat was regarded as the highest of the Yagnas where one would become a **Chakrabarti Samrat** after it. **Uchhashrava** represents the seven layered heaven, earth & underworlds and giving away its lordship in charity to **Vamana** Avatar of Vishnu just like king Bali did.

7. Once **Vishnu** is given the highest of the charities the native becomes his ardent devotee or bhakta and submits his true soulful love unto him which then adores as **Kaustabha** or the most valuable divine jewel offered to Shri **Vishnu**.

8. Once the bhakta completely submits to the almighty lord his only desire to live transforms completely to divinity of service & becomes the tree of **Nishkam Karma** represented by the **Parijata** whose roots are deep down his nature. Through his **Vairagya** the earthly form of the native remains always evergreen and never wilts.

9. The power of the **Vairagya** creates a powerful raj yoga in the native. This yoga creates a strong

foundation for a combination of sharp wit, intelligence & agility. Thus, with the power of **Vairagya** one can easily assume victory over the truth & justice which is represented by the powerful bow of **Sharanga** by which Shri **Vishnu** won over Lord **Shiva** as an archer. _The native thereby possesses an intellectual deep insight of skillful projection of his neutrality over truth for the purpose of preservation of the equilibrium in this universe._

10. Once the **Vairagya** of the native achieves the complete neutrality of the truth over his actions, thereby he is blessed with the power of manifesting any of his dreams, desires & wishes as a complete form of immediate reality without any delays or disappointments. This divine attribute is represented by **Kalpavriksha**.

11. Once the native achieves **Vairagya** over his karma through **Nishkam Karma** he achieves complete victory over all his senses & all forms of his incarnations, reincarnations. This is represented by the **Shankha** or the conch of **Vishnu** which echoes the vibration of the victory of _reincarnation over immortality_.

12. Once the vibration of the victory of _reincarnation over immortality_ is echoed by the **Vairagya** of the native his true consciousness arises from the depths of his several reincarnations. This consciousness is so pure that it is qualified of being part of the crown of truth or **Lord Shiva**. _This pure consciousness of the Yogi arising from the kundalini is represented by the **Chandra** which bejewels the crown of the_

13. Once pure consciousness of the native arises, he becomes free of all diseases & ailments. This is represented by **Dhanvantri** the divine physician or the god of good health & shows freedom from all diseases. With complete freedom from diseases and any forms of ailments we can achieve complete happiness and enjoy all the happiness of the truth of immortality of several lives within this single life or incarnation.

14. The **Amrit** holds the secret of the immortality of the soul over our reincarnations & depicts the truth of the principle of Purusha & the Prakriti over this universe all other parallel universes beyond.

*Thus, this complete lifecycle knowingly or unknowingly, voluntarily, or involuntarily is a complete dance of **Natarajan Mahadev** or agitated **Kundalini**. Therefore, perhaps it is wiser to accept this life as a dance of kundalini and manage it accordingly.*

With these key concepts discussed any truth seeker will be able to organize their lives and will be able to segregate its true nature from unnecessary distractions & toxins arising because of the cosmic churn of their vast inner ocean of consciousness.

Thus, ends this chapter on the role of **Kundalini** over self-realization.

13.   Heaven, Hell, and the Demigods

Every human being long for the highest state of bliss in the world. As men wonders where the paradise is & what is it, a truth seeker emerges inside him. These emotions arise whenever his heart is unable to find the true state of bliss in his existence and observes several imperfections around this material world of the living.

His attempts to seek for paradise further complicates his mind and distracts him of the probable happiness he could have received out of his little satisfactions that he obtains out of his sense gratifications in the human society. Slowly he loses his peace of mind in the quest of the paradise and forgets everything around him and cares little for those around him. He then expresses deep remorse that this world is not perfect and then his concerns slowly replace his little satisfactions.

Finally, someday these human beings dies & leaves the known world around him, his grieving relatives behind & fails the almighty to create a better world around him in search of the paradise. What can be the greatest irony of life than this is!

However, the question here is does god really wants the truth in this way and did our quest for truth not supposed to help us in finding the bliss while we are living. Are we not responsible for trying & creating a better world around us rather than searching for a paradise? Well, the answer should be Yes, we are all entrusted to shape this world better and make others feel good about it. We all should be morally responsible & caring for others so that we ourselves can & help others to live a paradise on earth through self-introspection and constantly struggle to improve and transform ourselves.

Therefore, at the beginning of the chapter on the discussion of heaven & hell it was important to understand the background of the human emotions which sets the stage for the human mind longing for paradise & despise the burning fires of the hell.

Now first we will try to define what heaven is & how do our human minds comprehend about it. To some people heaven is a world of complete bliss, to some it's a world of complete happiness & pleasure, to some it's a world of complete peace, sanctity & purity whereas to others it's a complete world of emotional security & achieving the infinite tenderness, calmness & healing which makes it an absolutely desirable place called home. Therefore, the reflection of paradise in this material world is our dream home.

We all are working hard to make our homes a dream home to live the paradise on the earth. Home is our daily resting place, & a grave is our final resting place.

Home liberates us from the bondage of the daily work and provides us rest & peace and offers us the safety of our beds to sleep. Therefore, a home provides nutrition and emotional security like a mother. Its for this reason that fourth house in astrology is attributed to the home or the place of residence & to our emotional securities & mother. Its also attributed to our motherland & our roots or the country of our origin. The fourth house is the first **Moksha** house due to the rest & tranquility it offers and therefore signifies the paradise around us.

The astrological fourth house is also the house of our immovable possessions that we strive to bring into our lives. These possessions can be both material as well as spiritual in nature. Therefore, if there are any astrological afflictions in the birth chart on the fourth house or its lord of the native, his paradise is lost from him. It depends on the nature of the affliction from the birth chart that we can comprehend whether the paradise will be restored. If there are any benefic aspects on the affliction the paradise will be restored around him. Most often these individuals become wanderers in search of paradise and home. Its because of these wanderers that explorers and saints are born, and they can restore not only the paradise around themselves but can also create one for others by healing them.

The astrological eighth house signifies our final resting place as per our birth culture & religion once we exhaust our longevity is in this life. It can be initially mean a grave or a crematorium. Therefore, the eighth house is the second **Moksha** house.

The eighth house being the second **Moksha** house also indicates the afterlife and our existence in the astral plane. It is the house of the rebirth and spiritual transformations during this life and lives beyond. Therefore, the eighth lord and its nakshatra are two most important things to determine the afterlife and our astral existence in the afterlife.

While studying and researching on Vedic astrology I have always tried to focus and discover the secrets hidden behind the Nakshatras.

The lunar mansion in Vedic astrology is divided into twenty-seven nakshatras.

Each nakshatra indicates a unique constellation with different stellar systems on them.

There are twenty-seven presiding deities corresponding to each of these nakshatras and this is not just a correlation. Each of these nakshatras therefore indicates the abode of these deities indicating the highest and the lowest forms of metaphysical spiritual life corresponding to these nakshatras.

In the Bhagvada Geetha Shree Krishna himself mentioned that in the nakshatras he is the **Abhijeet**. This nakshatra is not part of the 27 constellations and this is the only nakshatra which is not feminine. This distinguishes **Abhijeet** nakshatra from the rest of the 27 nakshatras.

Every mythological story has a hidden meaning encoded in them. The story of the 27 nakshatras and their relationship with **Chandra or Moon** also has a hidden meaning. The mythological legend says that **Prajapati Daksha** the son of **Brahma** had 27 daughters whom he got married to **Chandra Deva** and instructed him to love his 27 daughters equally. **Chandra Deva** however was more affectionate towards **Rohini** therefore **Moon** which is the planet of the **Chandra Deva** has been observed astronomically to slow down a little bit more time at **Rohini** nakshatra and spend relatively more time there than other constellations while the Moon is orbiting around the Zodiac in his lunar mansion. Therefore these 27 nakshatras signifies the 27 daughters of **Prajapati Daksha** & signifies the gateways to 27 different cosmic worlds. In one of the earlier chapters, we have discussed about the seven upper layers which are the heavens & the seven lower worlds which are the underworlds. Therefore, there are total fourteen lokas or fourteen cosmic worlds. In the **Garuda Purana** Lord Vishnu very clearly talks about the abode of **Yama &** the human accessible heavens to either enjoy fruits of good **Karma** or suffer the fruits of sinful **Karma** and from the astrological studies

We know that **Yama** is the ruling deity of the **Bharani** nakshatra.

Astrologically **Bharani** is the nakshatra of the rebirth and transformation therefore the portal to **Yama Loka** is located in the **Bharani** nakshatra. Similarly, **the Pitris** or the ancestors are the ruling deities of the **Magha** nakshatra. Therefore, the portal to the **Pitri Loka** is located in the Magha nakshatra from which our guardians or the ancestors look over the earth. Therefore **Pitri Loka** & the **Yama Loka** are two of the heavens. For grouping the nakshatras into fourteen Lokas we will have to consider a 28 nakshatra system including the **Abhijeet** nakshatra which is the abode of **Lord Shri Krishna** and is the portal to the sacred **Golak Dhama.**

When **Brahma** started creating the worlds, he also created time. Scientifically time can only exist whenever there is a relative periodic circular motion or there is a relative periodic wave motion. Thus, when Brahma started creating the upper worlds within the universe, he aligned them in a complex architecture so that their layered alignment looks like an elevated imaginary invisible mountain which is mentioned in the Puranas as **Mt. Meru.** This **Mt. Meru** is the actual **spiral** galactic alignment of the upper universe in the form of inclined, elevated & trunked concentric **spiral** paths. Therefore, it cannot be seen through telescope or naked eyes. As we calculate **Kalpa** & **Yuga** time cycle on the earth all the galactic system alignment in the form of **Mt. Meru** relatively is rotating around their central stars and further greater central stars in the form of a spiral and eventually around the **Brahma Loka** or the abode of **Brahma** which is the origin of the spiral. Similarly, the seven lower galactic worlds are aligned in the form of an inverted mountain called **Mt. Mandar.** The search for cosmic truth ends at **Garuda Purana** where Shri **Vishnu** answers and clarifies all our anticipated FAQs to his devotee and universal carrier **Shri Garuda,** the king of the birds. **Shri Brahma ji** has designed & created this human body & its subtle Chakras in replication to the design of the actual **Kalpurusha body** or the universal form of **Lord Shri Krishna.**

Therefore, the external cosmic truth which we are scientifically pursuing through astronomy, astrology, or space research all their answers are hidden and encoded internally within us. The day we will uncover all the truth inside us, our quest will end there, and we will realize that reincarnation is the only truth, and it happens as per the will of the Lord. That day all our relative desires becomes completely insignificant & meaningless before the universal desire and the will of the Lord.

In the **Garuda Purana Shri Vishnu** mentions to meditate upon our seven upper chakras to become aware about the locations & subtle characteristics of the seven Lokas above us. Similarly meditating upon the seven lower chakras below the **Muladhara** we can become aware of the seven lower worlds. This is a hidden message for the explorers & truth seekers. Those who understands this hidden message will be able to decode & further understand the truth that the universal alignment in the **Kalpurusha body** is the exact replication of the human **Chakra** system.

189

For the purpose of recollecting about the seven upper worlds including the earthly plane below is mentioned the facts about them.

- **Bhūloka-** The sphere of the earth or Bhūloka, comprehending its oceans, mountains, and rivers, extends as far as it is illuminated by the rays of the sun and moon; and to the same extent, both in diameter and circumference, the sphere of the sky (Bhuvarloka) spreads above it (as far upwards as to the planetary sphere, or Swarloka). Wherever earthy substance exists, which may be traversed by the feet, that constitutes the sphere of the earth (Bhu Loka). 'Bhu' means 'Earth' and 'Loka' means the surface of planet Earth, where we live.

- **Bhuvarloka-** The region that extends from the earth to the sun, in which the Siddhas and other celestial beings move, is the atmospheric sphere (Bhuvarloka). Bhuvarloka is identified with Earth's atmosphere and sometimes with the space which is in the immediate neighborhood of Earth.

- **Swarloka-** The interval between the sun and Dhruva, extending fourteen hundred thousand leagues, is called by those who are acquainted with the system of the universe the heavenly sphere (Suva Loka). Suvaloka (alternatively Swarloka) is beyond Bhuvarloka. Some description makes it a planet inhabited by the Devas with their king Indra. Some references make it equivalent to the Swarga. Some Puranic references equate Suvaloka to the Solar System.

- **Maharloka-** Above Dhruva, at the distance of ten

190

million leagues, lies the sphere of saints, or Maharloka, the inhabitants of which dwell in it throughout a Kalpa, or day of Brahma.

- **Janarloka-** At twice that distance is situated Janarloka, where Sanandana and other pure-minded sons of Brahma, reside.

- **Taparloka-** At four times the distance, between the two last, lies the Taparloka (the sphere of penance), inhabited by the deities called Vaibhrájas, who are unconsumable by fire.

- **Satyaloka-** At six times the distance (or twelve Crores, a hundred and twenty millions of leagues) is situated Satyaloka, the sphere of truth, the inhabitants of which never again know death.

These three lower spheres are termed transitory: the three highest, Jana, Tapa, and Satya, are styled durable: Maharloka, as situated between the two, has also a mixed character; for although it is deserted at the end of the Kalpa, it was not destroyed yet.

Based on these facts we have grouped the Nakshatras into the Seven upper Lokas or the heavens aligned in **Mt. Meru.**

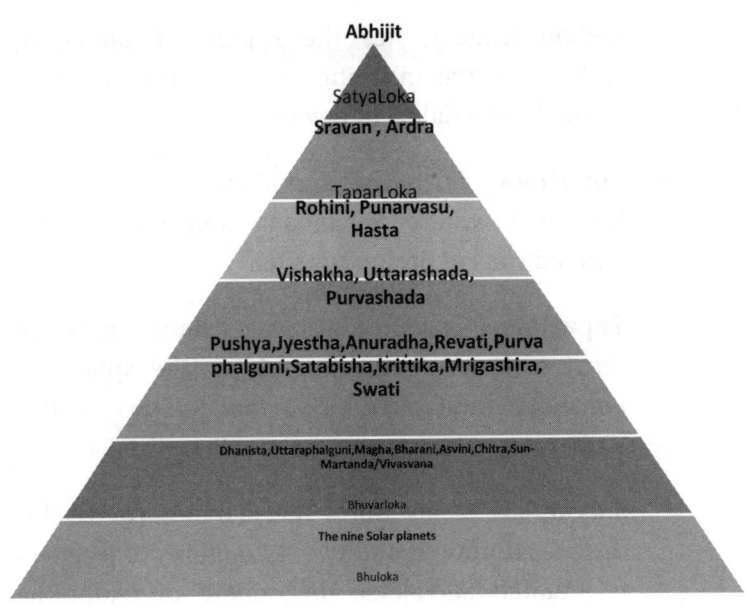

Basis of the above grouping is below.

- **Satyaloka** is the abode of the supreme personality of god head.

- **Taparloka** is the abode of great sages born out of Vishnu, Shiva is the Adi Yogi or Tapaswi.

- **Janarloka** is the abode of complete purity i.e., Brahma & Savitri.

- **Maharloka** is the abode of gods who can move in a Kalpa to either Brahmaloka or to Swarloka or the Heavens.

- **Swarloka** is the abode of Adityas like Indra, Varuna, Soma & Mitra along with Dev Guru Brihaspati.

- **Bhuvarloka** is the abode of the Pitris & Aryaman the first of the Pitris. The Vasus or the gods of the earthly abundance along with Yama the god of righteousness are the divine beings who resides between the Deva Loka and the earth and are in close proximity with the earthly beings like humans. Chitra is the abode of the celestial architects like Maya & Vishwakarma. Ashwini kumaras twins are the doctors of the Devas and are the sons of the Sun god who is the eighth Aditya known as **Vivasvana** or **Martanda**.

The complete list of Adityas or the suns of Aditi owning stars:

1. Varuna deity of Satabisha

2. Mitra deity of Anuradha

3. Aryama deity of Uttaraphalguni

4. Bhaga deity of Purvaphalguni

5. Savitr deity of Hasta

6. Tvaṣṭar deity of Chitra

7. Indra deity of Jyeshta

8. Martanda / Vivasvana our Sun

- **Bhuloka/Martyaloka** is the abode of our earth and earthly planets like Jupiter, Saturn, Mars etc. There are also other earthly planets inhabiting this layer in other galaxies. The term **Martyaloka** has ascended from **Martanda** our Solar deity. Therefore, **Martyaloka** is our Sun and its planetary system. **Bhuloka** on the other hand refers to all the other earthly galaxies that has life on them. Therefore, **Bhuloka** is an extension of **Martyaloka** and can be considered as a superset of it. **Brahma** created replica galaxies like ours to spread the illusion of human life being inhabited on other planets. Thus, **Bhuloka** is a collection of endless scientific pursuits for world inhabited by humans.

Through the above classification as mentioned in the **Bhagvada Geetha** we are not denying the existence of the aliens. The reason for non-denial is also **Bhagvada Geetha** which mentions about the seven lower worlds beneath the **Bhuloka**. These lower worlds are inhabited by non-humans & creatures that has often invaded earth and its human settlements. The upper worlds & their occupants are the protectors & guardians of this earth & solar system. The references of the non-human alien invasions are found in almost all the mythologies. In the Mahabharata a fierce **Gandharva** named **Chitrangad** came to earth and challenged the king of same name who was **Shantanu** & **Satyavati's** son & **Bheesma's** cousin in **Hastinapur** in a dual & killed him.

Chitra is the constellation of celestial architects, craftsmen, musicians & artists. **Gandharvas** are the celestial musicians and artists and they often used to visit earth for recreation. Their temperament however is not the best and are often of very base nature.

Due to this nature, there has often been conflicts between them and the humans. Besides the above reference there is another reference in the Mahabharata which states that the Gandharva king **Chitrasena** (*Chitra + Sena*) came to a forest on earth.

After the Pandavas lost in the dice game of the gambling and went on for exile, Duryodhana planned to humiliate Pandavas by showing them the luxuries enjoyed by all the Kauravas and Karna. So, all of them had set to forest where Pandavas were living.

In the course of Journey, Duryodhana abducted a lady without knowing that she was a Gandharva princess & daughter of **Chitrasena**. Then the Gandharvas headed by **Chitrasena** attacked entire Kauravas and Karna. Kauravas and Karna got defeated. Karna tried run away from battlefield after getting defeated by Chitrasena, but he couldn't since Gandharvas captured all Kauravas and Karna. On knowing this, Yudhishthira asked Arjuna to free them since its their lineage which would be insulted. Arjuna followed his eldest brother's order and first requested **Chitrasena** to release Kauravas and Karna. Chitrasena rejected and asked Arjuna to fight with him in order to free Kauravas and Karna. Thus, a battle took place. Arjuna defeated many warriors & captured **Chitrasena**.

The name **Chitrasena** itself which is a combination of **Chita** & **Sena** suggests that this **Gandharva** was the commander in chief of the army of **Chitra**. **Chitra** is the constellation inhabited by the **Gandharvas**. Thus, every mythological name in Sanskrit is not an individual but a designation and signifies the identity of the individual or of the origin. The constellations and their deities are given below in the tabular form.

Nakshatra	Constellation Lord	Constellation Layer	Reason of Classification
Abhijit	Shri Krishna	Satyaloka	Krishna is the ultimate truth or Satya beyond all universal truths. Thus, Golakdhama is in Satyaloka.
Sravana	Shri Vishnu	Taparloka	Taparloka abode of great sages born out of Vishnu. Thus, Vaikuntha is in Taparloka
Ardra	Shiva		Shiva is the greatest Yogi or Tapaswi. Thus, Shiva Loka is in Taparloka.
Rohini	Brahma	Janarloka	Brahmaloka is the abode of complete purity where Brahma & his mind sons reside
Punarvasu	Aditi		Aditi is mother of all celestial gods and wife of Kashyap, the son of Brahma. Dev Mata's residence & position is above all Devas/Adityas.
Hasta	Savita		Savitr mentioned in Gayatri Mantra & Rigveda is the Aditya, the first sun god & resident of the Brahmaloka. Savitri or Gayatri or goddess Saraswati is the divine goddess of knowledge and wisdom and the Gayatri Mantra describes Savitr as her light. Therefore, Savitr is the cosmic star of knowledge & his light is the wisdom that reaches to us from the Brahmaloka.

Vishak ha	Indragni or the king of heavenly fires.	Maharlo ka	Two forms of fire attend the Creator: Agni soma and Indragni. These are the two forms of fire required for religious rituals. Agni soma is at Brahma's service so that the Creator can have health and vitality (the principles of Soma) to live as long as the creation. Indragni is at Brahma's service so that he can obtain divine intelligence and power by worshipping Vishnu. Indragni is the foremost of the primordial heavenly fires & is the fire used in sacrifices and rituals. Thus, Indragni is the god of ritual fire.
Uttaras hada	The Visvedevas or universal gods		From Indragni emerges the power of invincibility for collective consciousness. Thus, from Visvedevas Brahma can create the divine collective consciousness of the devas that can make them invincible for the protection of the universe.
Purvas hada	Varuni/Apah universal goddess of water		Fire & Water are complementary of each other and thus are the Ashada nakshatras. Apah signifies all sorts of divine water including rains & is the goddess of complete invincibility with the power of the divine waters.
Pushya	Brihaspati the Guru of	Swarlok	The Deva Guru resides with the devas in the heaven and guides

197

	the Devas	a	them
Jyeshta	Indra the King of the Devas		The foremost of the Devas resides in Indra Loka one of the heavens
Anurad ha	Mitra God of devotion & friendship		Indra, Mitra & Varuna are the favorite of the brothers in the Adityas
Revathi	Pushan the God of nourishment		Divine nourishment residing in the heavens providing nourishment to devas and humans
Purvap halgun i	Bhaga God of love & marriage		Marriage is a divine law of the heavens and binds deva couples as well as human couples together as per applicable laws for both
Satabis ha	Varuna God of night sky & underworld		Varuna is the Indra on duty during Dakshinayana or winter solstice which is the night of the devas
Kritika	Agni God of heavenly fire		Heavenly fire residing in the heavens used for rituals performed by the devas
Mrigas hira	Soma God of nectar		Soma, the ultimate liquid; ambrosia of the gods which grants unsurpassed health and enjoyment.
Swati	Vayu God of Air		The most powerful god without which life cannot exist on earth
Dhanis ta	Eight Vasus or Gods of earthly	Bhuvarlo ka	Controls primordial earthly elements They are like they ray of light expanding from the

	abundances		*Supreme: Earth, Water, Fire, Air, Sky / Space, Sun, Moon, and Stars*
Uttara phalgu ni	*Aryama an Aditya foremost of all Pitris*		*Foremost of all Pitris & an Aditya who is one of the guardians of the earth*
Magha	*Pitris or the guardians & the ancestors*		*The guardians & the ancestors staying closely above the earth & often visits through astral bodies*
Bharan i	*Yama God of death*		*Yamaloka the residence of Yama where mortals are judged post departure of souls & grants them fruits of their Karma.* *This becomes both the heaven & hell for Jivatmas as per the good or bad Karmas that they perform in their lifetime. Good Karmas enjoy the heavenly pleasures granted by Yama in his abode & bad Karmas had to suffer punishment in his dungeons.*
Ashwin i	*Asvins or the twin God of divine medicines*		*Twin sons of the Vivasvana or Sun god who are the celestial doctors*

In the **Garuda Purana** the details of the hellish sufferings as per the sinful & forbidden Karmas given by Yama are clearly & unambiguously explained by Shri Vishnu. We are not discussing them in detail here.

The classification of the cosmic nakshatras as per their temperament are given below.

- *Gentle & Divine Temperament*- *Ashwini, Mrigashira, Punarvasu, Pushya, Hasta, Swati, Anuradha, Sravana, Revathi.*

- *Moderate & Earthly Temperament*- *Bharani, Rohini, Ardra, Purvaphalguni, Uttaraphalguni, Purvashada, Uttarashada, Purvabhadrapada, Uttara Bhadrapada.*

- *Cruel & Impulsive Temperament-* *Kritika, Ashlesha, Magha, Chitra, Vishakha, Jyeshta, Moola, Dhanista, Satabisha.*

Having discussed the detail of the various heavens & explained the concepts of the Hell and mentioning about the different demigods corresponding to each heaven we have reached at the end of this chapter. Thus, end our chapter on the Heaven, Hell & the demigods.

14.   The Divine & The Demoniac forces

In the light of the context of the forces it is remarkable to note how **Brahma** created the various worlds within the universe and balanced their inter as well as intra equilibrium. He implemented forces like gravity, magnetism, electromagnetism, centripetal, centrifugal as well as nuclear forces at the atomic level to establish stability & equilibrium at the molecular levels of consciousness. At the organic levels of consciousness, he organized these atoms as carbohydrates, complex proteins and further organized them to form living cells consisting of **DNA** & **RNA**. At an inorganic levels of consciousness this passion for stability created new elements.

His engineering as well as the mathematical designs implementing torque, time, frequency & thermodynamics are flawless and worthy of worshipping. However, **Brahma** is not worshipped due to a curse given by Lord **Shiva**. **Brahma** generated **Savitri** or **Saraswati** from the primordial elements of Knowledge, Wisdom & conscience. However, **Brahma** himself ever thirsty of pure knowledge wanted to take Saraswati as his consort and tried to persuade her. Since **Brahma** generated Saraswati therefore she was his own daughter and thus it was sinful to marry his own daughter. Therefore, **Shiva** cursed him and took away his pride of being the foremost of the generators or the most revered creator of the worlds. All the universal forces are forms of **Shakti** and therefore should be attributed to Lord **Shiva** who is the primordial static form of all cosmic forces. Lord **Shiva** is the **Adi Purusha** & therefore is the better half of **Mother Adi Shakti** the primordial dynamic form of all cosmic universal forces. Therefore, any sinful acts towards any forms of **Shakti** will generate the wrath of Lord **Shiva** and the sinners are bound to get destroyed.

At the atomic consciousness level **Sattva** or Proton is associated to **Vishnu, Tamas** or Neutrons following neutrality is associated to **Shiva** & **Rajas** or Electrons following the passion of molecular bonding is associated to **Brahma.** Therefore, **Brahma Shakti** is the power of the electrons or its electronic charge; **Shiva Shakti** is the power of the neutrons or its neutral charge & **Vishnu Shakti** is the power of the protons or its positive electric charge. If these concepts are clear, then the world can be perceived perfectly as the dance of different forms of **Shakti. Brahma** not only implemented his **Brahma Shakti** to design the worlds but also implemented **Psychic** forces like Greed, Anger, Lust, Pride, Deceit, Irreligion, Envy & Fear to bring about instability & chaos in his created worlds which can drive his creations to passionately look for more stability in their **Rajasic** world. **Brahma's** creations are bounded by their defined duties & inner **Rajasic** nature to their worlds. Thus, the **Rajasic** nature of the creatures and the **Tamasic** rule of their communities binds their duties towards the growth of such communities.

When a creation of **Brahma** follows this path, he fulfills his duty towards his creator, however due to **Brahma's** psychic forces he remains passionate and becomes sinful. Thus, such an individual gets trapped into a continuous cycle of reincarnations and rebirth to fulfill his passions & desires. However, the one who is entitled to enlightenment will know that surrendering himself unto the **Sattvic** nature is the only way to reduce the effect of **Rajasic** shakti in his life. Those who surrenders slowly discovers the divine within themselves & becomes devotees. One who enters the mode of devotion by the grace of god their intellect and minds gets purified and they do their daily work under the guidance of their conscience. Once conscience awakens it invokes consciousness and by working through this world the devotee performs his duty. Not once he gets separated from the lord as he is always completely immersed in his thoughts and those thoughts convert into actions. By doing such devoted actions he gets devoted reactions and fulfills his destiny in this world.

Now what are the human attributes by which we can identify who are the devotees and who are not? Only the **Sattvic** devotees can transcend and release divine energies. This is where the devotees of Shri Vishnu are constantly engaging in chanting his name and does every work remembering him so that their energies connect. By doing this they are automatically pleasing goddess **Yogamaya** who exists as goddess **Lakshmi**, the consort of Vishnu. Therefore, they receive peace & prosperity in their lives. Goddess **Yogamaya** is the creator as well destroyer of all worldly illusions. Therefore, Sattvic devotees are aware of the truth that this world is an illusion created by **Yogamaya** and she forever stays in their enlightened mind and prevent devotees getting attached to those illusions throughout their lifecycle. The devotees just focus on doing their work & they don't do their work for the purpose of getting rewards. They get rewarded by her as per & requirement when the fruit of the time ripens.

The **Rajasic** devotees are capable of releasing passion and hence can be either divine or demonic. This is where the demons try to please **Brahma** and asks for immortality out of their ignorance. The wise & the enlightened worships mother **Saraswati** who is the consort of **Brahma** & gets her blessings in the form of knowledge, wisdom & spiritual intellect. This helps to balance the passion of **Rajas** & also pleases Lord **Brahma**.

Tamasic devotees can transcend to **Sattvic** after a complete heart transformation & that's what the **Shiva** Bhakti leads to. Therefore, a devotee of Shiva has to automatically please Mother **Shakti** the consort of Shiva in order to please him as well. Lord Shiva & Mother **Shakti** are the Father & Mother of this universe known as **Jagatpita** & **Jagatmaata**. Therefore, if a devotee's heart is childlike and pure, they get the blessings of both of them. **Jagatpita** Lord **Shiva** protects every devotee as his child and being **Mahakal** or the controller of time himself Shiva knows the future and the past of the devotee as well. If Shiva is not happy by the destiny of his devotee as written by **Brahma,** he can mysteriously take the tests of the purity & integrity of his **Bhakta** and by his will can change it through the power of his forgiveness. Such is the divine grace & power of **Jagatpita**.

With the divine grace of **Lord Shiva & Shri Vishnu** & their energies integrated was born **Bajrang Bali Shri Hanuman** in Treta Yuga. In **Kalyuga** human beings will have their intellectuality at the lowest level as said by **Goswami Vedvyasa** ji to understand that the cosmic reality of Vishnu & Shiva is both same as a photon. One represents the particle nature whereas the other represents the wave nature. Therefore, in Kalyuga **Shri Hanuman** will be the primary protector of saints as per Shri Rama's boon of being Chiranjeevi or immortal in this **Kalpa**. Therefore, those who chants Hanuman Chalisa will receive the protection of Shri **Hanuman**. They will reclaim their intellects which has a possibility of otherwise getting polluted by **Kalyuga**. When they are able to retain their intellects, they will be able to understand **Bhagvada Geetha** & thus follow <u>Universal Religion of humanity, hope & Faith</u>. Thus, Hanuman ji is the protector of Sanatan Dharma on this earth in this dark age of **Kalyuga**.

Kalyuga symbolizes the rise of the demonic psychic forces inside human beings which we will discuss in the next chapters. Therefore, it is important to identify what are the demonic psychic forces which Bhagvada Geetha very clearly mentions about. Identification is the first step & the second step is to transform them into divine qualities. With the power of the **Bhakti** the second step can be achieved however difficult it might be. **Bhakti** or devotion creates faith and faith invokes will power inside the human beings. Therefore, nothing is as powerful in this universe than the positive faith of a devotee on his god. Those who doesn't understand the above and blames god for all their earthly sufferings becomes further engulfed in evil and becomes slaves of the demonic psychic forces within themselves. They become further food to external demonic influences and thus transforms into those individual followers who sustains demons.

In this age of social media, we understand that any leader divine or demonic gets their power from their followers. The more the followers the more the powerful they become. As the Bhavisya Purana written by **Goswami Vedvyasa** says **Kalyuga** is the age where leaders and leadership positions will be occupied by corrupted people and only the followers of greed, corruption, cruelty, lust & selfishness will gradually rise to leadership positions in the second phase of **Kalyuga**.

They will rise quickly and will become the greatest source of misery and downfall for their followers. Evil & biased political leaders will rule their countries by evil laws and gradually spread the corruption at all levels. Mobs may hijack the powers as we can see in the drawback scenarios of democracy & republic. Non-believers of faith & Irreligion as well as their followers may create more chaos & might tactfully occupy leadership positions of powerful nations. These are some of the prophecies of the **Kalyuga** which we can see are already coming true.

In the Bhagvada Geetha Shri Krishna explains Arjuna below which means Pride, arrogance, conceit, anger, harshness, and ignorance-these qualities belong to those of demoniac nature.

Dambho darpo bhimanas ca

Krodha parusyam eva ca

Ajnanam capabhijatasya

Partha sampadam asurim

The **Bhagvada Geetha** is an ultimate source of identifying self-improvement parameters towards a nearly ideal life full of bliss. In the modern world we are inventing different technologies for helping people improve their lifestyles. Trade & commerce have become globalized & slowly currencies & their managements have become more digitalized. Seldom do we realize how such huge money is circulating over the internet and ecommerce businesses. The rich are getting richer and the poor unable to completely understand the formula of currency conversions and the mantra of success are getting addicted to the world of internet. In today's world computer literacy is must to create and manage assets. Those who doesn't understand it will become irrelevant and wipe away. In such a volatile age where the multiplication is the success mantra, we are in the first five thousand years of **Kalyuga** which is its golden period. There was a legendary story in Mahabharata where King Parikshit the grandson of Arjuna met **Kalyuga**. He allowed **Kalyuga** to reside in four places- **Gold, Prostitutes, Alcohol & Gambling**.

From this symbolic story it is clear therefore that **Kalyuga** will have huge amount of wealth. With the ease of buying & selling, corporates & social media have captured the electronic & commercial market. Information is a commodity now and every data is important. Therefore, predictability of human behavior & habits is analyzed using captured data along with high usability of artificial intelligences to speed up the business processes. This rapid creation and generation of huge wealth and assets will lead to further extensions in the creation of jobs. This will force people to land on more competitive edges in the job markets and almost all the sectors like Agriculture, Manufacturing, Natural Resources, Food, Utilities, Garment, Furnitures, Groceries, Real estate, Entertainment, Media will slowly become corporatized. Small scale traders will cease to exist in the market as they won't be able to compete with the corporates.

Larger corporates will take over smaller competitors. These

corporates and social media will become so strong that they will start controlling the governments and will eventually decide the fate of democratic & republican countries. They already have specialized Legal & Marketing Teams to assist them in their growth and once they become king makers law and order will become pawn in their hands. They will negotiate with the governments to the best of their interests. Thus, they will turn the gradually growing populations of the world into corporate slaves. We have just seen a trailer in the form of East India Company taking over India & neighboring countries. We called this colonization in history. With growing population, it will be difficult to provide agricultural lands to support such a huge population. Therefore, almost all populations will slowly turn into meat eaters. Therefore, the prophecies of **Bhavisya Purana** are likely to come true.

Average longevity of mankind is already seen to get reduced due to pollution, stress, and other factors. Rahu is therefore the king of **Kalyuga** among the nine planets. Demons like **Tripurasura** have been forecasted to take birth in Kalyuga by **Bhavisya Purana** to reclaim their glories. During this dark age men of religion & wisdom will become lazy & irreligious thus paving way for demonic forces to take birth in such families. Wealth will slowly become the only parameter to judge the goodness of a human being.

Kalyuga is the age of demon **Kali**. Now let's see what the **Kalki Purana** tells us about the birth of **Kali**. After the annihilation, the secondary creator of the universe, Lord

Brahma, the grandfather of everyone, who was born on the universal lotus flower, created Sin personified, having a black complexion, from his back. The name of Sin personified was Adharma. The wife of Adharma, (Irreligion), was named Mithya, (Falsehood). They had a son named Dambha, (Pride), who was always very angry and energetic. Dambha, had a sister named Maya, and within her womb, he begot a son named Lobha, (Greed), and a daughter named Nikrti, (Cunning). Lobha begot a son named Krodha, (Anger), in the womb of Nikrti. Himsa, (Envy), was Krodha's sister. From the womb of Himsa, Krodha begot a son named **Kali**. Now to end the age of **Kalyuga** Lord Vishnu will take the incarnation of Lord **Kalki**.

He will be assisted by all the divine forces of the universe to restore righteousness, peace & justice.

Thus, end this chapter on the divine & the demoniac forces.

15. Kalyuga & The Role of Human Beings in This Complicated Age

Before we started this discussion, we have introduced the concept of **Kalyuga** in the earlier chapter. We have also discussed about the four yuga cycles that follow in the previous chapters. In this chapter we will discuss briefly about the symptoms of **Kalyuga** as narrated in the **Shrimad Bhagavatam** and how can an average human being counter them. We will also discuss some benefits of **Kalyuga** inspite of being a dark age.

The **Kalyuga** or the dark age symbolizes that phase of the mankind where a human being will have to face their own inner demons at its peak. The six evil attributes of greed, lust, anger, pride, jealousy, delusion will be at their peaks. Instead of four wheels the vehicle of righteousness will stand & run at only one wheel. Money will become the only parameter to judge the mode of goodness of a human being. The learned and the wise leadership of the societies will indulge in sinful acts. The administrators of the land will become more corrupted. Pollution will reach its peak and human population will have to suffer enormously dealing with natural calamities. The families will no longer remain joint and will degenerate into further nuclear families. Human beings will suffer from multiple chronic diseases and will become bereft of good health & vitality. There will be impurity in every basic survival need starting from food, clothing, medicines, shelter & services. Loyalty will gradually decline & all kinds of ethics including political, civil & work will be at its lowest level. A human being will eagerly wait for another to die in order to usurp their possessions. There will be innumerable wars leading to death & destructions. Longevity of mankind will be at its lowest level. These are some of the important symptoms of **Kalyuga**.

Now the most important question: What is the benefit of Kalyuga?

Shrimad Bhagavatam mentions that although **Kalyuga** will be the darkest age still there is hope for all those who are devotees and retain their faith on the Lord. **Bhakti Yoga** or the devotional service to the god will provide the required intellect and the wisdom to survive through this difficult time and attain liberation. Through **Bhakti Yoga** a devotee will work directly under the guidance of the lord so that he can better manage the challenging times and at times be forgiven for committing mistakes knowingly or unknowingly. In this age of Kalyuga most of the sages and other saintly human beings are found to be born with **Vipreet Raj yoga** in their birth charts astrologically. The reason is under adverse circumstances the best of such individuals will come out and they will be able to manage any difficult circumstances positively with their approach and at the end ensure the victory of the righteousness.

Therefore, **Kalyuga** is certainly difficult to manage, however provides with a unique opportunity to leave behind examples of positive leadership, faith & wisdom under tremendously difficult circumstances.

If human beings realize in this complicated age that all the foreplay & events of the universe are occurring to motivate them to uplift their spiritual growth along with their materialistic developments, then they will be able to establish a balance and create long term assets that can benefit the progress of the mankind. **Kalyuga** offers the most wonderful among the administrative systems in the form of republic and democracy. If these systems are compared with all the forms of medieval systems of monarchy then we will find that republican system offers respect for all individuals, religion and practices that can uplift human spirit and take them to next levels of **Karma Yoga**. If we can make the best use of these systems, we can build a reflection of paradise on the earth. Time & often reformers are born who will help to improve the progress of the system and by contributing to reformation we can help in building a better world.

Therefore, by understanding that the game of creation as played by **Brahma** under the supreme guidance of Shri Vishnu & Lord Shiva is just their fantastic plot to motivate us to find a simplistic way to them. Sometimes through adverse circumstances we get an opportunity to discover the best of the potential among us & therefore the first five thousand years of **Kalyuga** poses that opportunity to discover the hidden and the best of the potential among us. It will definitely lead the human beings to discover the best in them through their sweat and tears. Therefore, the ideal way to cross the vast ocean of the material world in this age of **Kalyuga** is to ride on its back. The journey will often be difficult, adventurous, challenging & adverse however one with complete faith & surrender to the lord will find at the end that the complete journey was simply a magic woven to test their faith. One will find himself lying at the lotus feet of **Shri Rama or Lord Shiva or Shri Krishna** whoever he believes in when the spell breaks.

Therefore, lets walk under the protection of our faith, sing under the devotion of our love, and dedicate our lives under the guidance of our conscience. We will find that the lord speaks through our conscience & works through our consciousness.

If we perform our duties without any expectation & practice loving each other through compassion & care, we will find that our role on this earth is limitless. By helping each other to heal we will be able to build human societies which are sustainable, healthy, and prosperous. By creating assets, we will be able to wipe off the tears of the poor & needy.

By imbibing kindness among the human beings of different races, religion, cast & culture we will be able discover that we all are children of the same god. We might give different names as per our understanding & teachings of our prophets and gurus for his different cosmic forms however the truth remains the same that all the paths of a true religion led to the same cosmic truth which we might experience differently in different forms in our lives.

Therefore, no religion can be above humanity and the religion of humanity. Therefore, **Universal Religion** or **Sanatan Dharma** is above all religions as it preaches the above principles and leads us to believe that we as human beings can be the masters of our own destiny by our faith, devotion, love & respect for all individuals irrespective of their background and origins.

By practicing the principles of **Universal Dharma,** we achieve perfection over all the psychic forces and among tremendous risks attain capabilities to transform them into opportunities. The greatest desire among all of us is to see the best of each of the individuals among us. It could be our family, friends, relatives and all the folks of the society and our community itself. The fact that we all are earthly beings doesn't make us perfect. If we are completely trusting someone our trusts are sometimes broken too. We then start blaming others for breaking our trusts and confidence. Sometimes we forgive them too. However, the fact remains same that we all trying to discover god in his human form all over around us. Therefore, our subconscious mind prepares parameters as per its knowledge and experience to find an ideal figure among us.

Our sense of perception longing for a perfect relationship tries to find stability and security in all of them & sometimes in this quest our faiths are broken, and our confidence & inner peace shattered. Seldom do we realize that we all are earthly human beings, and our earthly expectations are leading us towards attachments.

Any kind of attachment is delusion and hampers spiritual progress as it leads to Karmic attachments & blocks liberation of the souls. Therefore, the spiritual attachment force as created by **Brahma** is governed by **Rahu**, he is an expert magician who traps us in our own illusory views of the world known as **Maya**. **Ketu**, on the other hand acts like the opposite pole of the magnet and causes detachment from our **Karma** & illusory views of the world.

Rahu creates tremendous longingness for any person, place or thing and drives us to go for it and grab it under our possession. **Rahu** drives us to break any social taboo or culture and considers the conservative views as indecent, inferior, and complex. It can lead to tremendous crisis in order to break the societal rules, beliefs & practices. It creates strong passion that drives us to adventure and break any rules. It derives us fun from breaking rules. Thus, in extreme cases it can lead to commit serious crimes & sins

215

and the person under **Rahu's** influence can discover himself suddenly under the scan of the local authorities and the law enforcement agencies.

Rahu drives an individual to earn wealth through dishonest and corrupted means and when its cycle is over can flip the card over to **Ketu** who then shows the individual his true mirror and often the individual under his sense of guilt fails to find any solace in the wealth he has earned. Then finally enters the scene the universal judge **Saturn** who summons the individual & passes his judgement to sentence the individual and provides justice to his victims. Therefore, all sorts of money laundering, gambling & prostitution are performed under the influence of **Rahu**. However, when the card flip overs to **Ketu** often they start feeling empty suddenly under the scanner or guilty. If they admit their sins and tries to heal themselves through reformation and transformations, there are possibilities that they can be saved. The judgement passed by **Saturn** is often slow but sure.

Rahu is a pretender and often poses as a healer when **Ketu** is playing over his card and draws individuals into addictions. **Rahu's** promise of healing is through addiction in all intoxicant forms like alcohol, tobacco, or any other forms of addictive ingredients. It can be through food, habits, views and infact anything. When **Saturn** enters the scene in the above scenario, he gives serious punishments to the individual to modify their habits and leave behind their addiction. Under the joint influence of **Ketu and Saturn** the individuals detach from their addictions and turns spiritual. In **Kalyuga** this is a common phenomenon where we can see many rehabs & ashramas working dedicatedly turning such addicted onto saints and performing yoga & other austerities under the guidance of a guru.

Their spiritual progress is slow but sure. As they find more people like them whom they consider as the victims of the destiny around themselves they are able to co-relate to the same pattern of committing mistakes and finding an opportunity to revive themselves after an initial suffering. Thus, **Saturn** purifies everyone at the end and revives them through practice of extreme penances & sacrifice.

Rahu & **Ketu** are thus the kings of **Kalyuga** & **Saturn** is the magistrate & the instruments of jury & law. **Mars** becomes another important instrument in the game of **Rahu** & **Ketu**. **Rahu** utilizes **Mars's** aggression & rage to drive individuals to commit crimes. **Mars** becomes **Rahu's** general in **Kalyuga**. His combined effect with **Rahu** leads to political henchmen, gangsters, smugglers, and all sorts of money extortioners in this age of **Kalyuga**. Thus, in this age of **Kalyuga** naturally we will find that astrologically **Rahu** & **Ketu** becomes more powerful than the luminaries **Sun** & **Moon** and can have adverse effects on the soul if the position of both the luminaries are not strong in an individual's chart. **Mercury** becomes the advisor or the minster of **Rahu** & **Ketu**.

Rahu utilizes **Mercury's** intellect to create wealth and assets through the instruments of either corruption in negative circumstances or in positive scenarios through innovations and automations or even sudden scientific discoveries. **Rahu's** combination with **Mercury** is sufficient enough to drive the intellect of a human being to achieve their passion. Its effect is synonymous to the story of **Kalyuga** where King **Parikshit** allowed him to reside in gold and thus **Kalyuga** occupied the gold crown on his head and turned his intellect against his wisdom. Thus, I have tried explaining in detail astrologically the most difficult topic of the unpredictable & malefic natures of **Rahu & Ketu** prevalent over **Kalyuga** and what are their instruments.

Now let's try to discuss the beneficial effects of the same **Rahu & Ketu**. **Rahu** drives any forms of experimentation, research & exploration, corporate houses, innovations, and commercial ventures of scientific nature & pursuits. All accidental and sudden scientific discoveries in the history of the mankind have been motivated by the power of Rahu. While **Ketu** decides over the impact of those important scientific discoveries in the forms of commercial utilities & their side effects. For example, in this age the most important contribution of **Rahu** is the discovery of the computers and wireless technologies. While these innovations have led to the substantial creation of employments across corporates & through internet has connected the entire globe and communities across it.

Rahu's automation has been a catalyst in boosting global business and trade along with wealth multiplication and creation of assets. However here the seamless nature of **Rahu** in providing ease of business and services through the combination of **Mercury and Saturn** has driven **Ketu** to simultaneously act in the favor of rise of taxes, essential expenditures & loans to such an extent that inflation is arising at a rapid rate.

The rise of inflation can detach us from affordable housing & other utilities.

Due to inflation higher bank loans, credit cards and other commercial financial debts are fast becoming a trend in today's world. The innovation of airplanes its

218

commercialization through corporate airlines along with the discovery of the television and internet are all motivated by the airy, electronic & wavy nature of **Rahu & Ketu**. Therefore, we all are significantly exposed to the effects of **Rahu & Ketu** in this modern times and therefore its important to understand how these psychic forces operate in our lives. Constant exposures to **Rahu & Ketu** are like exposures to radioactivity which can severely damage the functioning of our lives in the long term.

Therefore, the exposure must be handled with something like radioactive shields and other instruments to save guard ourselves from the harmful effects of the exposure in this age of **Kalyuga**.

Rahu rules over all sorts of addictions over mobiles, computers & internet and when digital technologies and currencies are fast replacing manual methods and transactions its important to understand that diseases and internet frauds are also rising as commanded over by **Ketu** to detach us.

Therefore, the alternate cycles of attachment and detachments will continue through the cycles of new software & technical inventions, software updates, which will further drive us to expose their bugs, speed, performance and detach us from their backdated utilities in the ever-changing world of the commercial demands.

Thus, directing the inner Rahu & Ketu towards Bhakti Yoga paves the path for liberation. Now with Bhakti Yoga one will be constantly under the guidance of the lord and the direction of his attachment will only be towards god. Thus, at the beginning we might have to give some difficult & tricky tests which proves our faith and trust on god. When our inner **Rahu** gets convinced of our pure devotion, he will go to meditation & will invoke the power of the truth or the Shiva Shakti within us. Inner Rahu is an ardent devotee of lord Shiva and once he goes into a state of meditation, he invokes the third eye chakra within us. During this phase of inner Rahu, we might experience some mystic events which will further invoke inner Ketu to drive us towards the detachment of the physical reality around us.

As we get detached from the physical reality under the influence of the inner Ketu the meditating Rahu will steer the soul towards the metaphysical realm and our soul might experience the metaphysical universe existing around us. This process is known as the process of the enlightenment or the Sadhana where one becomes completely aware of the existing metaphysical world around themselves. With the Bhakti Yoga and increased focus, the soul becomes guided by not an earthly human guru but comes directly under the guidance of the supreme lord. The soul under such a state of consciousness becomes free from all ignorance and realizes that nothing happens without a cause and that all psychic forces and incarnations of God are operating towards motivating the entire human race to realize the truth and becomes free from all sorts of attachments, illusion & take shelter directly under the will of the god.

Thus, whatever age, whatever place, and whatever time if an individual realizes that they are born by the will of the lord, whatever they are doing are by the will of the lord and whatever they are gonna do are also by the will of the lord. His life, his death and his further reincarnations are also decided by the will of the lord and by the knowledge of this process alone he becomes aware of the truth and accepts the metaphysical reality in this Karmic world. His rising conscience becomes capable of healing himself, purifying himself as well as share his knowledge and heal others and motivate them towards the same realization and liberation. Thus, that devotee gets automatically liberated from the clutches of the illusory **Kalyuga** and the timing of their reincarnations are probably to occur as devotees & associates of **Lord Kalki** when he transcends this earth to end **Kaliyuga.**

16. The Virat Rupa of Lord Krishna

Finally, it is giving me immense pleasure to present the cosmic form of Shri Krishna as per the Bhagavad Geeta so that we can visualize this world and the entire humanity as one and together as a universal family. The cosmic purusha & the principle of inclusion constitutes the Virat Rupa of Lord Shri Krishna.

The Yogi who has completely submitted to the devotion of the lord sees the entire universe and all the creatures in it as one, He is not separate from it either and thus this realization brings him closer to the Lord. Inclusiveness alone constitutes the Virat Rupa & if in modern age we request Shri Krishna to show his universal form, I am sure he will show us the great **United Nations Charter & constituent assembly** as a demonstration of his Virat Rupa at Country Group Level. Virat Rupa is a Global & Universal constituency. Students of the cosmic science who believes in the inclusiveness of all religions and understands the core of the Universal Religion concept should understand that by meditating on Virat Rupa of Shri Krishna alone their quest for truth ends. Virat Rupa in the modern age means that all Gurus, Prophets and Religions lead to the same universal truth, however through different procedures, techniques, practices & principles. **Division & Integration** are two principles of the same universe that drives the growth & sustenance as well as the saturation & destruction of it. They are the two faces of the same coin. Therefore, differential & integral calculus must be applied simultaneously to understand the principle of Virat Rupa.

When Arjuna requested Shri Krishna to show his Universal form in Kurukshetra, The Lord showed this cosmic form to his ardent devotee and friend Arjuna. This form will be incomprehensible to ordinary human beings as its infinite and shows all the universe & beyond in its truest & finest cosmic form. If we can visualize & decode the meaning of the Virat Rupa of Shri Krishna it becomes easier to discharge our duties along with developing an understanding of our role in this universe. Thus, seekers of the truth with the visualization of the universal form of the lord gets closer to the truth. When they get close to the truth their mind stops seeking further and thus, they get liberation. This is the sole reason for which Shri Vyasa included & described the Virat Rupa of Shri Krishna to constitute the Bhagvada Geeta so that devotees can attain **Moksha** through **Bhakti Yoga** alone in Kalyuga.

Deepest philosophies are born from the Deepest Crisis. Without Detachment there is no Liberation, without desire there is no reincarnation, Without Pain there is no healing & Without search there is no truth. Only the Love of Prambrahma detaches & liberates, Only the Selfless love leads to final truth.

If one believes in inclusiveness this entire universe belongs to them. If they believe in exclusiveness nothing is theirs. The primary question that comes to the mind is can someone detach themselves from their material existence for an entity/being which they have never seen or heard?? **"Nirakar form"** or they can just do their Karma considering their love for the unseen and unheard so that they can express his divinity in this world in the form of his followers, speech, and action? So, they built a temple and worshipped him in his **"Sakar"** form. They offered him obeisance in the form of flowers and fruits and kept his photo to feel his presence around them.

This is a classic example of **Karma Yoga** realized through Bhakti. Seldom do we realize that our thoughts, actions, feelings, and emotions all arise like the waves in the ocean of the cosmos made of Sattva, Rajas, Tamas. Our desire or Rajas is driving us, our attachment or Tamas is binding us and our search for truth or Sattva is calling us!!!

By the power of the Bhakti, the Nirakar takes Sakar form. Its because of this shakti the Prambrahma manifested into creator, preserver, and destroyer viz the Brahma, Vishnu and Mahadev to continue an infinite cycle of creation, dissolution, and recreation. To demonstrate this system and its universal inclusiveness the Prambrahma himself took birth as Shri Krishna on this earth. His Virat Rupa is a message to all those understands him and wishes to understand him that inclusiveness is the only principle that has kept the Dharma of humanity alive on this universe.

All the Prophets, Gurus & messengers rise by his order & by his order alone they perform their Karma on this earth. No Prophet, Guru or Messenger or their followers are above the will of Shri Krishna.

Human Beings are perhaps the only creatures who stands face to face in a conflict caused due to ideological differences among their leaders. Therefore, one must choose their leaders carefully and as per the rules of Dharma. If we look at the history of mankind, we will observe that all the ideological conflicts which led to warfare were caused by the extremists and leaders who held extreme visions and views about time, society, and mankind. Only moderates and their thoughtful ideologies to reconcile leads to peace, prosperity, and wisdom. Shri Krishna by his Virat Rupa demonstrated this principle to his devotee and Bhakta **Arjuna** in the battlefield of Kurukshetra before the beginning of the war.

He first narrated to **Arjuna** the principles of **Samkhya Yoga, Gyan Yoga, Karma Yoga and Bhakti Yoga.**

He then enlightened **Arjuna** on the universal principle that leaders who follow extremist ideologies are bound to create conflicts and clash among themselves because of their extreme views. The principle of moderation, negotiation and peace keeping fails with them. Therefore, these leaders along with their followers are bound to get vanquished as per the universal laws of dissolution and recreation. They don't follow the path of Dharma which leads to humanity and peace.

As **Shri Krishna** says the below sloka in the Bhagvada Geetha which means Dronacharya, Bheeshma, Jayadratha, Karna, and other brave warriors have already been killed by me. So, slay them without being disturbed. Just fight and you will be victorious over your enemies in battle.

dronaṁ cha bhīṣhmaṁ cha jayadrathaṁ cha karnaṁ tathānyān api yodha-vīrān mayā hatāṁs tvaṁ jahi mā vyathiṣhṭhā yudhyasva jetāsi raṇe sapatnān

By this sloka alone **Shri Krishna** says everything about the laws of Karma, time (Kala) and destiny (Niyati). What he says here is noteworthy and should be followed carefully by every person who is aspiring to be a leader or is already a leader. **Shri Krishna** here gives a direct message that the fate of these great warriors itself were decided in those moments when they decided to disrobe a royal woman of her honor, by engaging in gambling & other vicious dishonorable acts & tried to win the wealth and people of a great nation which was built on the principles of Dharma and by the sweat, blood & sacrifices of its people. Nations are built by its people and leaders. Those elders who without a protest led that act of Adharma happen to such a great nation and its tradition such elders and their fates were also decided in that moment itself. When the Leaders become dacoits and gamblers their fates are also sealed in that moment or Kala itself. This is what Shri Krishna perfectly meant. By his order in that **Kala** itself **Mahakal** or **Lord Shiva** prepares his plan to send his vultures to feed and feast on the dead bodies of such leaders and warriors in the battle fields along with their followers.

When **Shri Krishna** showed his infinite Virat Roopa which was incomprehensible to Arjuna he shut down his eyes in fear. The **Virat Roopa** was as bright as the light of thousand Suns shining together. Arjuna previously prayed to **Shri Krishna** to show him his true divine form and when **Shri Krishna** did out of his benevolence **Arjuna** soon realized that he as an ordinary human being has limited capacity like that of a tiny drop of sand in front of an entire desert. He then requested the lord to forgive him and come back to his human form. Hearing **Arjuna's** prayer **Shri Krishna** returned to his human form. Its by the wish of Lord Shri Krishna alone that I am writing this book and by his wish alone what I have heard from my Gurus and ancestors I will try to write a few words on his Virat Rupa that can best describe the universal aspect of the lord.

The three aspects of the Kala or the time viz the past, present & the future resides in the universal form of the Shri Krishna. The Panchabhoot elements, Ether, Ego constitutes the layered dimensional elements of his material & spiritual body. The Lokas and planes of existences constitutes his external organs. In divine form Indra and other Devas of light are his hands and Agni is his mouth, Sun God his eyes, Vedas are his Brahma Randhra, Objects of affection are his teeth, His enchanting smile is Maya, infinite creation is his side glance, his lower lip is shame, and his upper lip is greed. Dharma is his chest and Adharma his back. Brahma Prajapati is his generative organ and Mitra and Varun Gods are his sense of taste. The oceans and seas are his belly, mountains his bones and rivers his veins and arteries. The trees are his hairs, and the powerful wind god is his breath. Time is his movement. His play or Leela is the flow of Guna. Prakriti is his heart and his Manas or emotion is moon which is the source of all transformation. Mahat is his perception & Shiva or Rudra is his Ahamkara or Ego. Therefore, the supreme Purusha constitutes the Ego or Ahamkara of the Virat Rupa. Gandharvas, Apsaras, Vidyadharas and Charanas are his musical notes and Asuras are his strength.

In human form The Brahmins are his mouth, Kshatriyas his hands, Vaisyas his thighs and Sudras are his legs. The Devas are his sacrificial Ghee and Yajna is his Karma.

Thus, the vast and infinite Virat Rupa constitutes the universal cosmic system of the Prambrahma, and **Shri Krishna** was the only one to give a glimpse of it to Arjuna. By meditating on this Virat Rupa we realize the truth behind our existences and beyond it. By meditating on this Purusha we invoke the Purusha within our heart. We see his glimpse in every living and every subtle creature around us in this material realm. The third eye chakra awakens and a Sadhaka becomes free of all fears. Life, death & reincarnation is realized as a journey by the order of the Lord. Truth seems transparent like a movie on 32-inch projector screen. Dreams become realities and realities becomes a dream. The infinite Universe becomes finite like a tiny grain. We expand and our consciousness expands, when it unites with Krishna the consciousness becomes infinite and calm like the Pacific Ocean. This infinite consciousness is the ornament of **Lord Shiva's** head and hence **Lord Shiva** is also known as **Chandrasekhar Mahadeva**.

The one whose Yogic consciousness is infinite and such Shiva-Krishna (*Hara-Hari*) consciousness is achieved by realizing that infinite consciousness through union with the consciousness of **Shri Krishna**. It's for realizing the same consciousness and becoming **Chandrasekhar Mahadeva; Lord Shiva** meditates on **Shri Krishna,** and he sees **Shri Vishnu** the universal preserver & his Gunatit form in his heart. This love and Bhakti are what is demonstrated by **Lord Hanuman** when he tore open his heart and to everyone's surprise who was there, it was his & ours dearest **Maryada Purushottam Lord Shri Rama**.

Now in this chapter I will also try to explain that why **Shri Krishna** while teaching **Bhakti Yoga** explains the importance of complete surrender undo him for attaining infinite bliss. It is notable that even though after listening to the discourses of **Bhagvada Geetha** from **Shri Krishna, Arjuna** still had left in his heart some weakness to act on the battlefield. His grief was not completely overcome by the discourses of **Bhagvada Geetha**. He was still under the pseudo influence of the earthly ignorance and affection towards his relatives. Therefore, he requested Shri Krishna to show him his divine appearance. With partial surrender none can overcome their ego and thereby partial surrender gives birth to doubt. This doubt can then become a major roadblock or challenge for even the God to enlighten his **Bhakta** or devotee. This poisonous tree of doubt & ego can then only be overcome by the axe of curiosity and complete surrender.

The act of complete surrender invokes the attribute of faith and thereby gives it a right direction for the God to enlighten his devotee and liberate him from all ignorance, suffering and pain. **Shri Krishna** the almighty knew this and hence instructed **Arjuna** to overcome all his weakness of the heart which were a major roadblock to discharge his duties as a **Kshatriya** or a warrior in the battlefield.

Therefore, **Kurukshetra** becomes a **Dharma Kshetra** or the spiritual field of righteousness and self-discipline not only because of it going to host the historic battle of **Kauravas v/s Pandavas** (righteousness & true rights v/s tyranny & deceit) but also because every warrior here was fighting an inner battle within themselves of overcoming their spiritual weaknesses and ignorance with the true knowledge & wisdom of righteousness and the path to the divine. Those who were exploring the purest option of self-realization and rectifying their spiritual mistakes which are a major roadblock to selflessly discharge one's duties towards the mankind, themselves, their country, and the universe stands with the **Dharma**. Those whose personal agenda and self-realization was through the path of Ego, Self-Satisfaction and sense gratification were not with the **Dharma**. For both these parties **Shri Krishna** acted as a mirror.

Those that did not stand with **Dharma** Shri Krishna led them to self-realization by teaching them that those who loses the battle within and fail to win over themselves also loses the physical battle outside.

They are doomed and their destinies lead to only death and destruction and rather not peace and prosperity. **Shri Krishna** by becoming the charioteer of the spiritual chariot of **Arjuna** vanquished the unrighteousness and the tormentors of the humanity. He invoked their Self-Realization through vanquishing them that led them to the path of liberation from false ego, anger, lust, and ignorance caused due to passion.

For those standing with Dharma like in the case of **Arjuna**, **Shri Krishna** enlightened them by winning over self that would lead them to the transcendence and eternal bliss through self-realization of the nature of the atman and its true cosmic connection with the paramatman. This divine relationship with the **Prambrahma** is established by **Shri Krishna** when he instructs **Arjuna** and emphasizes on the importance of complete surrender unto the God known as Bhakti Yoga that leads a Bhakta to liberation from all ignorance within and ensures their victory and transcendence over self through the knowledge of the self-realization.

Therefore, I as a servant of **Shri Krishna** humbly & completely surrender unto him and pray to him that he leads all the readers of this book to eternal bliss, peace & prosperity through the path of Self Realization. By Continuously chanting **Hare Krishna, Hare Rama** we become united with the energies of **Shri Krishna and Shri Rama.** They become our Guru in this process of Bhakti Yoga. When the God himself becomes our guide there is but a guarantee of only one thing and that is enlightenment. Thus, with this prayer ends this chapter on Virat purusha and I take shelter unto him in this chapter of the book.

17. The Significance of the Care & Love of Cows in the Sanatan Dharma

Swami Vivekananda the first Yogi who traveled to the west once said in his native mother tongue Bengali *"Jibe prem Kare jei Jon, sei Jon sebichey Ishwar"* which means the human being who has loved another living creature has served God. This universal love and compassion are the basis of the Universal Religion. A Yogi always loves and nourishes the idea of caring for other creatures whether humans or animals. When Shri Krishna used to play his flute in the Vrindavan all the creatures including the cows, birds, snakes, and other wild animals used to get mesmerized by the charm of the divine music and in the process used to long for the eternal companionship of the Lord. When the Lord subjugated & danced on the fangs of the notorious serpent Kaliyah Naga who had threatened the cows of the Vrindavan the message to the world goes that we must protect the weak and the followers of the Dharma.

The message also means that those like who threatens the pious souls that nourishes the universe like the Cows are nothing but poisonous serpents of ego and arrogance like Kaliyah Naga. Therefore, Cows are under the eternal protection of the Lord Shri Krishna. There is a reason for which Cows are given special consideration in the light of the Sanatan Dharma. Their torment and slaughtering are a direct blow to the Dharma. Animal cruelty and slaughtering are the rising concerns in this Kaliyuga. Human Beings due to their selfish reasons has turned the animal slaughtering into a commercial business. Animal husbandry for slaughtering has become the basis of the commercial food business chain. Animals like humans are the creations of the God and often when we slaughter them in mass, we forget it. God is the protector for all its creations and therefore humanity suffers from Pandemics like Corona, Chicken Pox on account of these Sins.

There is a reason for which Cows occupies the core of the existence of Sanatan Dharma and that is not because of the commercial use of the dairy products. Clarified butter or Ghee is the purest offering to light the fire of the Yagnas and all dairy products are the result of the spiritual nourishing and healing energy of the Cows. The energy of the Cows heals and detoxifies all the toxic energies of the human body. Association with the cows scientifically has been researched and found that it purifies human mind and consciousness. This spiritual realization forms the basis of the Hindu Religion.

Killing of the innocent, Loving, and caring is not certainly a cup of cake for an enlightened soul. Butchering a creature whose eyes shower love and nutrition is the Dharma of the evil. These incidents can bring tears into the eyes of the saints and the awakened Yogis. The eyes of the cows are the mirrors of our soul. When you look in them you will find God and his divine love and benevolence for all his creations. A cow is all that a Brahmin the most enlightened one needs. A cow leads a Brahmin towards the divine. Cow is the connection to the divine. Therefore, religion says that the most valuable possession of a Brahmin is his Cows.

When the kshatriya Kings or the warriors in the ancient times planned to conquer the world, they used to select the rarest and most auspicious horse known at that time and perform Ashvamedha Yagna or the sacrifice of the fat of the

233

horse in the sacred fire. This horse was given in charity by the king who used to surrender to that aspiring Emperor. This horse was an embodiment of surrender v/s war. This horse was free to go wherever it wants and there was a complete army to protect it and its independence. Those that caught this horse insulted its independence and invited the wrath of the emperor. Thus, the war was for the protection of right of independence of a horse.

The warriors by proving their merit for the capability of protecting the horse ensured that the message is clear that in the reign of an emperor if just a horse is not safe then none of its subjects are. Therefore, a Kshatriya warrior after proving their merit for protection claimed the throne of an emperor. This was not an act of cruelty as seen in the west for criticizing the ancient cultures and conferred as an act of animal slavery and cruelty. Rather it was a way of proving the merit of the rights of the animals who used to serve the warriors in the battlefields. At the end of venture the Horse which stands for the victory of the rights of the animals were sacrificed to the Gods as a prayer and gratitude to them for rendering strengths to the warriors to protect them. This was an act of nature worship and not meant to feast on the animal. The fat of the animal was the only thing that was required to light up the fire of the Yagna rather than using the Ghee of the cow. The courage of doing this Yagna was not present in any ordinary king and only those kings who stands with Dharma and aspired to merge all the kings under his umbrella to create a United Kingdom used to perform this Yagna. Such an emperor could be found in only a hundred years. This was not a regular act of butchering and was not meant for feeding & feasting on the horse meet like the barbaric clans of the middle east and the Europe. Therefore, there is no question of animal cruelty in the

Ashvamedha Yagna as this Yagna stood for protection, justice, and rights of even the animals who served a kshatriya and none can look at them or even dared to steal them from a warrior when he was sleeping.

What Cows were to the Brahmins were the horses to the Kshatriyas. Therefore, religion prohibits a Kshatriya to feast on horse meat. Religion also prohibits to feed on boars as Vishnu incarnated as Varaha Avatar and lifted the earth out of the infinite waters & killed the demon called Hiranyaksha who has submerged it.

This story symbolizes the end of the aquatic age when the submerged land masses geographically came out of the waters and life thrived on them. Whenever the ice age ends then starts the melting of the ice due to global warming. Thus, begins the aquatic age when the continents get submerged in the oceans. This demon Hiranyaksha is nothing but the evil of the Global Warming on the earth. When the knowledge of the Vedas or the ideal lifestyle is lost to humanity it leads to global warming and green house effect. This evil then leads to the destruction of the mankind and hence is called a demon. The Vishnu or the protector of the nature then incarnates to protect the nature and the earth and recovers it so that life can once again thrive on the lands.

Therefore, animal cruelty has no place in the heart of the Sanatan Dharma. Sanatan Dharma stands for the love, nurturing, nourishment and protection of the animals and nature symbolized by the holy Cow. The elephants are the symbol of infinite wisdom, power, strength and symbolizes the victory of the protection of the Dharma and the destruction of the evil forces.

235

Therefore, Sanatan Dharma worships Shri Ganesh the embodiment of siddhis, divine intelligence, and wisdom. It's believed that Ganesh Ji wrote the Mahabharata on the request of the narrator Shri Vedvyas Ji or the compiler of the Vedas. He is the Son of the Shiva and the mother Goddess Parvati or the Adi Shakti which means that he is the offspring of the divine strength, wisdom, and yogic discipline. When someone connects with the cosmic energy of Shri Ganesh Ji impossible becomes possible. Beggars who are just spiritually so poor to only survive on the alms become kings or spiritual leaders who can lead & define administration of the world. Therefore, at the end of this chapter and the book I offer my prayers to Ganesh Ji to enlighten the world and keep on showering his blessings on the mankind. *"Om Ganpataye Namaha"*